An Indispensible Tool for the Understanding of the Hidden Meaning of Scriptures

3300 Hebrew and Greek words never before translated.

Dictionary
of
Biblical Symbolism

Compiled, edited, and with Introduction by

Stanislaw Kapuscinski

Published by INHOUSEPRESS, Montreal, Canada

ISBN 978-0-9731184-9-0

Other books by Stanislaw Kapuscinski:

Visualization - Creating Your Own Universe
Key to Immortality
Beyond Religion Volume I
Beyond Religion Volume II
Beyond Religion Volume III
Delusions—Pragmatic Realism

Table of Contents

FOREWORD
430 B.C.

Around 430 B.C. Democritus of Abdera said: *Nothing exists except atoms and empty space; everything else is opinion.* Today, some two-and-a-half millennia later, the same can be said of the Old Testament of the Bible:

Nothing exists but a lot of Hebrew words arranged in a linear fashion; everything else is an opinion.

Why? Because the ancient Hebrew had been written in capital letters only, in continuous lines without any breaks for paragraphs or punctuation. No proper names of either people or places had been identified in any way. All we have is a flood of words, flowing like a beautiful stream, perhaps a mighty river... *All else is an opinion.*

For centuries self-proclaimed experts imposed their opinion on what those words mean. In extreme cases, those who disagreed with the scholars approved by the Orthodoxy had been burnt at the stake. You needn't worry. In most countries murder and torture for religious belief is now illegal. Today, in most countries, you can dare to think for yourself.

And you must.

In the Age of Aquarius, religions, all religions, have entered a protracted, lingering period of inexorable demise. Dogmatic authoritarians are rapidly loosing their credibility. We have entered an Age of individualization.

We shall be forced to think for ourselves. It is with this sentiment that I am offering my Dictionary of Biblical Symbolism.

Everyone who so desires will be able to study ancient Scriptures and attempt to understand the secret, perhaps sacred knowledge, hidden in their pages.

And the knowledge of the ancients is staggering. On closer examination I found no evidence of any dogmas, no promises of unearned rewards now or hereafter, but also no dire threats of eternal damnation. But this is only *my opinion*. I shall not repeat the mistakes of the past by interpreting the Scriptures for you. I'm offering you the means to find your own wisdom.

The rest is up to you.

Good luck!

INTRODUCTION

The desert, near Nag' Hammadi
365 A.D.

As the dying wind sighed and heaved among the undulating dunes, a single dark shape, a hood pulled well over his face (the desert has many eyes), made its way towards the distant cliffs. Even from afar, brother El'zaphan could detect the agonizing whimpers of ghostly howling as it slithered low over the sand from the mountain ahead—the eerie mountain they called the Jobal al'Tarif. Its jagged slopes and contorted innards, ridden with countless forbidden caves and tunnels, held many secrets. For twenty-five centuries the dark, mysterious caverns guarded the scant remains of the noblest people. Perhaps some... not so noble. They said that the spirits of the unworthy howled, aye, howled and whimpered in the desert night air.

Brother El'zaphan shrugged his narrow shoulders. He knew better. He was among the few who shared in the Secret Knowledge. Soon the caves would serve once again as nature's sarcophagus to hold and protect the most noble remains. Those sacred volumes, or what remained of them, containing the Secret Knowledge which the inspired brethren had committed to papyrus. With such selfless love, such steadfast perseverance. At the risk of their lives.

And just as well.

The original Greek texts, those now translated into Coptic language, had been destroyed long ago. By whom? By the misguided ignorant men jealous of the secrets contained within the gospels. *"Gnostic gospels,"* they called them. *"Pseudo-knowledge!"* they sneered... *"The ravings of drunkards... Yes, of drunks and heretics... The knowledge of the devil!"*

Brother El'zaphan quickened his pace. His robe, the color of the whispering sand, gave him only partial protection from the lurking ungodly. He inhaled deeply. The cool night air filled his lungs with fresh strength after the scorching heat of the merciless desert sun. Yet the Books were heavy.

It wasn't far now.

Brother El'zaphan had been chosen go alone to Jobal al'Tarif, at night, and hide the thirteen books before the bishop's men made a burnt offering of them to their jealous god. Thirteen books containing more then fifty manuscripts that the scribes had consigned to paper with such determination. He, El'zaphan, had helped to cover them with the very best leather. To help them last. Who knows for how long?

"These are the secret words which the living Jesus spoke, and which the twin, Judas Thomas, wrote down."(1) His parched lips moved in silence recalling the sacred stanzas. He did not really need the Holy Books anymore. He had committed them all to memory. Long ago. But what of those who will follow?

It was only a question of time. Brother El'zaphan knew that ever since Bishop Irenaeus of Lyons had written his hateful dissertations some 200 years ago, calling for "The Destruction and Overthrow of Falsely So-called Knowledge,"(2) it would only be a question of time before the Orthodox Church, the fundamentalists, would lay their hands on his beloved Books and have them burnt as heresy. Ireneaus and his cohorts served a very jealous god.

8

Soon the Manuscripts would be safe. Safely hidden among the caves of the dead. The Books of Life, Logos, among the silent corpses. Even the orthodox priests and deacons were afraid to enter the hollows of the departed. The wandering spirits would protect the sacred stanzas from the ungodly. For as long as it took.
Until people were ready.

Give not that which is holy unto the dogs,
neither cast ye your pearls before swine,
lest they trample them under their feet,
and turn again and rend you.(3)

FOOTNOTES:
(1). *Gospel of Thomas,* gleaned from *The Gnostic Gospels* by Elaine Pagels, thereafter referred to as TGG.
(2). Irenaeus, *Libros Quinque Adversus Haereses* 3.11.9. Gleaned from TGG.
(3). Matthew 7:6; [*The Holy Bible*, King James Version]

Jobal al'Tarif
near
Nag' Hammadi

1945 A.D.

Many years have passed since brother El'zaphan risked his life on that lonely mission across the desert sands. Perhaps he was lucky. He had managed to avoid the needle of the deadly scorpion, the prying eyes of the Bishop's men and even the bandits who were ever ready to pounce on anyone within reach of that dreaded mountain, the Jobal al'Tarif. Even in his day some had dared to rob the graves of the departed. Perhaps brother El'zaphan had been lucky, perhaps under a Special protection.

Some 1580 years later, Muhammad 'Ali's mallet struck a tall earthenware jar. Quite by accident.

"Gold!" he exclaimed. Then, after glancing at his brothers, he bit his lips. He would have to share his find with them. In the name of Allah! Is there no justice in this world? His mallet struck the jar first, he must get the lion's share of the riches.

But there was no gold. There were just some books, wrapped in old-looking leather. But no gold. Perhaps he could sell them for a few piasters. If not, his mother could burn them in her cooking stove.

And his mother did burn some of the loose sheets. But only some. The rest must have been well protected. Just like brother El'zaphan.

It took another twenty-seven years before the first volume of photographic edition was released for publication. Nine more volumes were to emerge over the next five years. In 1977 the first complete, English language edition was published in the United States.

Perhaps it was meant to be that way?

We have now reached a stage in the history of the world when the whole of the human race as a body, or at least a large majority of people of every kind and of every race, are ready for the Second Coming of the Christ.... it is beginning to happen.... (it) is taking place now in the hearts of hundreds of thousands of people. (1)

"If you bring forth what is within you, what you bring forth will save you. If you do not bring forth what is within you, what you do not bring forth will destroy you" (2)

It would seem that the time is ripe for the next step in the development of the human psyche, or as the Bible prefers to call it, the human soul. About fifteen years ago, I came across some books written by the late Emmet Fox. I read them avidly. Later, I spent a good many years trying to find out if anyone had taken up the work, which Emmet Fox had began. I could find no one. I began looking for a dictionary that would explain to me the symbolism, which, according to Emmet Fox, served to conceal or rather to protect the mysteries of Truth and Wisdom, perhaps from those who might want to destroy them as heresy. The experience of Nag Hammadi had proven that whoever had chosen to leave over 3000 words of the King James Version of the Bible untranslated, must have done so for a good reason. I have not the slightest doubt, that if orthodox religions had the key to Biblical Symbolism, all the volumes would have been destroyed long ago as heresy.

Or altered beyond recognition.

Orthodoxy demands conformity and obedience and doctrinal conformity defines the orthodox faith. Effulgent diversity defines Divine creation. The two are at odds.

I have no degree in theology nor a doctorate in Divinity, though I had been offered the latter title, for $10 U.S. by post, when I visited Florida in 1982. I also lay no claims to divine revelations, though I believe that we all serve as channels through which the Divine reveals Itself to us. I do claim to have read a number of books and done some considerable research which, I hope, will serve the reader to look beyond the letter of the law and recognize the spirit thereof.

I offer no more than a few brief examples of the manner in which the Dictionary of Biblical Symbolism can be used, or applied to the original Biblical text. The examples are to serve as *illustrations* of how symbolism can be applied to unravel the allegories, and to increase our understanding of the original authors' intent. In my opinion the Dictionary works. Whether it will work for all the Books of the Bible, I have no idea. If not, I hope the readers will contribute additional information, which will augment and complement the work I have done to date.

I firmly believe that anyone who lays claim to possessing the final key to the total wisdom hidden in the Bible is both presumptuous and absurd. After all, those who will venture on this exciting journey of discovery should bear in mind that the Bible (Gk. *biblos*, a book) had been written by and for ancient people, living mostly in the Orient, under very different conditions and needs to ours and, perhaps most of all, *for people who could neither read nor write.*

The Books had been written in the ancient languages of Hebrew and Greek, the first of which did not even make use of vowels, as we know them, and the second of which few of the present day Greeks can understand. Furthermore, the Truth, or the deeper sense that the authors intended to convey, is hidden behind symbol, while the allegories are typical of *their* time, *their* customs and *their* spiritual needs. It has been said that Truth is One for all time. I have no intention to dispute this thesis but, if so, than I am sure that it must be constantly rediscovered.

It is my contention, however, that there *is* Secret Knowledge in the biblical writings. Furthermore and in spite of innumerable difficulties, the Truth seems to flow in great abundance to him, or her, who takes the trouble to look beyond the obvious. All too often the principle problem seems to lay not in the translation or the etymological origin of the word *per se*, but rather in our inability to rise above the belief in our own limitations to cope with such problems. But most of all, we seem to refuse to let go of our established mindset, our preconceived ideas.

Of one thing I am certain. Should we put as much effort into the pursuit of Truth, biblical or otherwise, as we do into almost any other facet of our day to day existence, we would advance on the scale of spiritual evolution at the same pace as we presently advance in physics, or chemistry, or medicine, or any branch of pure or applied sciences.

Principal Rules Governing Biblical Symbolism

There are very few such rules.

1. All the names of geographical locations, cities, towns, deserts, even houses, dwellings and tents symbolize conditions in which a soul may find itself at the particular moment when the story is being recounted. The names therefore refer to different *states of consciousness* the soul or psyche may enter on its path towards Self-Realization.

2. The personal names of the biblical characters, including their titles: mean *something*. There are over 3000 proper names (of places, tribes or individuals) in the Bible which *have been left untranslated*. Why? To protect the Truth? Possibly. In the Bible the name *always* describes or symbolizes the nature or the principle traits of character of the person so named.

3. The Bible appears to assume that every person on earth is an Individualization of the Infinite Consciousness. As such we all must define and express a *different* aspect of the One Truth. "We are all children of God".(3) Therefore, as there are no two identical blades of grass, it would be absurd to assume all souls are identical. We must postulate that each of us take charge of our own spiritual growth and find *our own interpretation* of those parts of the Bible, which are necessary for our *individual* development.

4. It is of absolutely no consequence whether the events or places described in the Bible have a "real" i.e. physical background or a recognizable geographical

location. Whether or not they are historically valid is of absolutely no consequence. Spirit knows neither place nor time. The interpretation of biblical symbolism and allegory neither denies nor confirms the "physical" meaning contained therein.

5. Often a number of actual or apparently divergent or even contradictory meanings are given for the same word. One of the reasons for such apparent confusion is that, according to the English translation, the same Hebrew word is used to name a mountain, a city, a man or a group of people. The student must decide if and when to apply any of the meanings suggested. [In my research, I also found instances where more than one Hebrew spelling is given for the same English translation].

The countless scholars responsible for the superb body of knowledge comprising the bibliography which often inspired, and equally as often confirmed my own years of study attest to a proven scholarship and erudition far greater than any to which I, or anyone *alone*, could aspire. Yet those diverse sources, *more often than not*, disagree on the precise translation of any particular word. In fact, on occasion, the sources provide either more than one possible meaning, or offer an answer with a question mark. And these gentlemen are acknowledged experts in the field!

Why such subterfuge? The Bible has been written essentially in two languages; the Old Testament in Hebrew, and the New Testament in ancient or classical Greek. Greek is a relatively easy puzzle to resolve, but Hebrew? To find the meaning of the Hebrew words the scholars had to reach back to etymological roots of over a dozen ancient languages. In my studies I came across references to: Akkadian, Arabic, Aramaic, Assyrian, Avestan, Babylonian, Egyptian, Ethiopic, Greek, Hebrew, Masoteric Text, Old Persian, Sanskrit, Syriac, Ugaritic...

I am sure the list goes on.

And even then, before the scholars could reach out to the etymological roots of comparative sounds, they had to decide on the Hebrew letters or phonetics. And that could not have been easy. The prophets may well have been divinely inspired, but the scribes were eminently human. Consider, for instance, that the Hebrew letters "y" and "w" (often transliterated as "i" and "u") are so similar in appearance and in the manuscripts are virtually indistinguishable.

But my work is not intended to baffle a curious reader. If the scholars could not agree on the 'correct' translation of any particular proper name, I decided to offer both, or three, or four of their best efforts. Whatever I accumulated over the years. After all, whatever the translation, the Dictionary is intended *to inspire the readers to discover spiritual truth*, not to impress them with the etymological roots of unpronounceable words.

The Dictionary does not necessarily offer the meanings but rather the ideas that the words, sites, places or people symbolize. I repeat that I am not in the least concerned with the geographical location of a city called Bethel, but with the symbol the word represents. The translation of the word Bethel is: *house of God*, but the symbol behind the meaning refers to a state of *raised consciousness*. Furthermore, I do not mean to imply that all the "names" must invariably carry a "hidden" meaning. More often than not, the translation itself provides the key to the spiritual intent of the inspired writer.

Finally, a word about the methods which many biblical scribes have used to protect their ancient revelations. For some reason there are people who imagine that although Jesus taught using, almost exclusively, the form of a parable or allegory, this teaching method was not known to the people of the Old Testament. These present-day adherents to orthodoxy [a somewhat questionable title derived from *orthos*: correct, and *doxa*: opinion] choose to retain their belief in spite of abundant references to the allegorical method of teaching in both the New *and* the Old Books of the Testament (see below). The Hebrews were always steeped in tradition, probably more so than any other race in the world. We can rest confident in the knowledge that if we cannot detect an allegory in the traditional Hebrew writings, than there is an excellent chance that we cannot, as yet, understand the true meaning of the scriptural teachings.

Let us at least try!

In the Old Testament there are no less then nineteen references to the use of parable as a tool for teaching. We find those references widely spread in the Books of Numbers, Job, Psalms, Proverbs, Ezekiel, Micah and Habakkuk.(4) But even this abundant proof is greatly surpassed in the New Testament. Here we find no less then forty-four references to the parable (Gk. *parabole*) in the gospels of Matthew, Mark and Luke.(5) The gospel of John avoids reference to the word as such, but not to the teaching method itself. Thus if we had any doubt that allegory or parable are the *normal* teaching methods employed in most if not all of the Bible, then surely, such doubts must now be totally dispelled. What remains now is to recognize the parables as such, then to interpret them. Judging by the literary output of the orthodox religions over the last one or two thousand years, no one will do it for us.

A question begs to be asked: Should the whole Bible be translated into a modern day language? *I most sincerely hope not!* To lose the flow of the inspired poetry, the lyrical beauty of David's Psalms, the sheer enchantment of so many stories told in the most vibrant allegories... to lose the thrill of great expectation... to lose all that—only to convert this compendium of mystery and vision into a dry, impersonal, long-winded, religious mystification would be a crime.

And after all, let us not forget what Jesus said some two millennia ago, when his disciples had asked him why he spoke in parables. His response: "Because it is given

17

unto you to know the mysteries of the kingdom of heaven, but to them it is not given."(6) Why?

Perhaps only a few were ready—then.

Before we plunge headlong into the new adventure, it is important that we all agree and attach the same meaning to the words: symbol, allegory and parable. Noah Webster defines them as follows: (7)

symbol, n. [Fr. *symbole*; L. *symbolum*; Gk. *symbolon*, a token, pledge, a sign by which one infers a thing, from *symballein*, to throw together, compare; *syn.*, together, and *ballein*, to throw.]

(further Webster definitions follow...)

allegory, n. [L. *allegoria*; Gk. *allegoria*, description of one thing under the image of another; from *allos*, other and *agoreuein*, to speak in the assembly; *agora*, a place of assembly.]

1. a story in which people, things and happenings have another meaning, as in a fable or parable: allegories are used for teaching or explaining.

2. the presentation of ideas by means of such stories; symbolical narration or description.

(other examples follow...)

parable, n. [O.Fr. *parabole*, from Latin *parabola*, from Gk. *parabole* from *paraballein,* to throw beside, to compare; para, *beside*, and *ballein* to throw.]

1. a short, simple story from which a moral lesson may be drawn; it is usually an allegory.

2. an obscure or enigmatic saying.

The King James Version of the Holy Bible defines a **parable** as a *religious allegory*.(8)

Having established the semantics, let us briefly consider the broader meaning of a 'symbol'. Is not every *word* a symbol? Is not a symbol that which invokes a certain image in our mind? If so, then the best I can hope to do is it to offer to you an "up-to-date" symbol with which you are conversant for one with which you might be less familiar.

On the other hand, the symbols employed in the Bible are of a universal nature, as though ingrained deep in the human psyche. We respond to them at a subliminal level, without conscious awareness. Or, as Carl Jung would have it: "a word or an image is symbolic when it implies something more that its obvious and immediate meaning." And later he qualifies: "As the mind explores the symbol, it is led to ideas that lie beyond the grasp of reason."(9) The ideas are not 'unreasonable', they go *beyond* reason, or as a student of the Bible could say, into the realm of the unconscious—onto the threshold of spirit. This is *the* principle reason why every person (who is interested in self-knowledge) must engage in their *own* interpretation of the Bible, as the unconscious is a personal, subjective, individual property of every man, woman and child.

Joseph Campbell issues a second warning. He asserts that: "Symbols are only the *vehicles* of communication; they must not be mistaken for the final term, the *tenor*, of their reference."(10) I choose to assume that Mr. Campbell refers to the communication between our conscious and unconscious mind. Perhaps even with our spirit, our Higher Self.

Today, the desert wind blowing from Nag Hammadi promises to raise the veil of mystery it has held for a duration. The powers of orthodoxy no longer wield the authority to burn a heretic [from Gk. *haireticos*: able to choose] at the stake, nor even to effectively threaten with fire and brimstone the soul which is ready to embark on the glorious path of self-discovery. Yet now, even as two millennia ago, we shall find that we all must make a very special effort. For the real veil hiding the Truth is neither in the desert sands, nor in the allegory nor symbol. It is drawn across our own eyes. Perhaps, if we try just a little harder, if we muster just a little more courage, if we have just a little more faith in the Silent Voice whispering in our soul, the mysteries of the Kingdom shall be given to us. As always, there is no free ride. I offer you the best key to the Pearly Gates I could find. The rest is up to you.

We have entered the age of Aquarius. The symbol of the age is a man watering his garden. His *own* garden. The garden of his own consciousness.

Good luck.

FOOTNOTES:

(1). Diagrams for Living by Emmet Fox,

(2). Eleine Pagels, The Gnostic Gospels. From the Introduction pg. xiii [Gospel of Thomas logion 70] Another translation: Jesus said: If you bring forth that within yourselves, that which you have will save you. If you do not have that within yourselves, that which you do not have within you will kill you. [The Gospel According to Thomas, Publ. Leiden E.J. Brill]

(3). Galatians 3:26;

(4). The actual examples are provided in the Analytical Concordance to the Bible, [ACB] on pg. 730

(5). Matthew 13:11

(6). pg. 98 of the CONCORDANCE; HB.

(7). WEBSTER'S New Twentieth Century Dictionary Unabridged, Second Edition,

(8). Matthew13:11

(9). Diagrams for Living by Emmet Fox,

(10). *The Hero with a Thousand Faces* by Joseph Campbell.

How to use the
Dictionary of Biblical Symbolism

I found that attempting to read the scripture while looking up the words in the Dictionary simply doesn't work. At least, not for a considerable while; not even with daily practice. Later it might, but frankly, once you know all the words that might have a symbolic meaning, you'll hardly need this book at all.

You'll go on—to the next stage.

But for those of us who feel, as I do, that we still have something to learn from the scriptures, I have prepared a few extracts. There is no special reason for the particular selection. I just opened the Bible at random and did the best I could with the verses before me. I kept the extracts short, because it is not my intention to influence anyone's interpretation. As is evident from the examples that follow, I stuck to a method that worked for me. I have typed the original text in bold. I then inserted the meaning or the translation I found in the Dictionary behind each word that I felt needed an explanation. [I used a computer. If you do not have one, you can use double spacing when you copy the text]. After a few paragraphs, I sat back and pondered a while. If I still could not understand what possible spiritual meaning may be hidden in the verses, I began writing in the right-hand column as best I could. Sometimes it took two or three attempts before the light dawned on me. On other occasions I wrote my 'interpretation' of the spiritual meaning as though it had always been obvious. And do not worry if a word or two is missing, or if one verse is less meaningful than another. It may be more meaningful tomorrow.

One other thing. If you can, I suggest you use the King James Version of the Holy Bible. Not only is it incomparable in its beauty, but it has fewer 'improvements' perpetrated by the learned scholars who perhaps searched for different knowledge in the very same pages.

The reason why the spiritual meaning seems, on occasion, so hard to perceive is that we have been taught, (surely most if not all of us) to rely, whenever and wherever possible, on the literal meaning of the scriptures, rather than to look for more than is immediately apparent. To do otherwise, we have been told, would be to play with the 'word of God'. To tinker with that which should not be tinkered with, perhaps to lose our good standing in whatever church to which we might belong and, what was by far the most frightening, to risk eternal damnation.

We can at least discount the latter. The Bible tells us repeatedly that the Divine Spark within us, our Higher Self, is an indivisible part of God. The Bible also assures as that God is Eternal. In all Its parts, regardless of creed or persuasion.

Yet it is not easy to *completely* reverse our attitudes which have been inbred into our subconscious, perhaps even genetically. And it might be hard to realize that progress is *not* limited to subjects dealing with all aspects of pure and applied sciences but *is* also possible to the science dealing with the Essence of our Being. "I make all things new", said the Son of man at the beginning of the previous area. Have you noticed that all things new are invariably condemned by the orthodox minds as the workings of the devil? And by devil I mean the 'beast' within us, our negative nature; the nature which seems to wallow in its own limitations.

Can anyone really believe that the Bible would have had such a profound, often subliminal influence on well over a billion people if the only meaning of the writings upon its pages was limited to the spilling of blood? The blood of sheep, and of lambs and of the heathen, of our enemies, of the unbelievers, the blood of children and their errant parents, the imprudent mothers and fathers, the human blood and even Divine? Would its pages remain an inspiration or perhaps an excuse for some of us to justify the mayhem and murder in the name of some 'higher' ideal? Surely, in this field even Mein Kampf has more to offer.

So why did the Bible survive the foibles of human nature? This question has been dealt with in the introduction. But why did the teaching survive all these years *in any form* in spite of the Crusades, the Inquisition, in spite of regiments of bishops blessing regiments of tanks facing each other on the battlefield?

The Dictionary is intended to help you to find the answer. But I strongly urge you. If you do embark on the journey of self-discovery, then look in the Bible *only* for that which you firmly believe applies to you, today, at this very moment of your journey. Don't act surprised if, in time, you will discover that all the books of the Bible have been written exclusively for your personal benefit.

Aren't you lucky?

APPLICATION

How to apply the
Dictionary of Biblical Symbolism

The Second Book of Moses:
EXODUS
Chapter 1: 1-14

(Original text in bold)

1. **Now these are the names** (traits which identify) **of the children** (soul(s) ready to embark on a new journey) **of Israel** (1) (he who is consciously seeking God), **which came into Egypt** (the land of material consciousness); **every man** (everyone) **and his household** (state of mind) (2) **came with Jacob** (the supplanter, following after)
2. **Reuben** (behold a son) (3), **Simeon** (a hearing, harkening), **Levi** (joined), **and Judah** (praise, praised),
3. **Issachar** (bearing hire, reward), **Zebulun** (dwelling), **and Benjamin** (son of the right hand, i.e. fortunate) (4),
4. **Dan** (judge), **and Naphtali**a (wrestling), **Gad** (the seer, lot, fortune, a troop), **and Asher** (happy) (5).

FOOTNOTES:

(1). Israel often represents 'a people', or a concept of one who actively searches for God. It the latter sense, all of us who embark on the conscious spiritual journey are Israelites.

(2). In a broader sense, "the household" defines the sum total of our mental and emotional development, including that which occupies our attention on a day to day basis, namely our present or immediate state of consciousness. It symbolizes that which in time will become a 'city'.

(3). In this case, the son symbolizes a "child", i.e. a new (higher or more advanced) state of consciousness. The awareness of such a "child" is the first step in our spiritual growth, which is dependant on our soul (psyche) giving birth to such new states of consciousness.

(4). Here son represents the more usual symbol i.e. "the result of" or "the consequence".

(5). All proper "names" represent nature or traits of character. The same applies to the names of "cities" only they define the broader concept of the diverse states of consciousness that our soul can enter (abide in).

(Application)

1. Now these are the traits of character, which identify a soul ready to embark on a conscious search for God, a soul that heretofore was marked only by material concerns. At this stage everyone's state of mind comes with the seed of that which is to follow,

2. —with the desire for a new state of consciousness, with the ability to listen to one's inner voice, with the commitment to a single purpose, with a grateful heart,

3. —with readiness to receive just rewards for one's efforts, with the ability to control one's state of mind, with being righteous and thus fortunate.

4. It comes with vigilant discrimination, with willingness to wrestle with one's weaknesses, with faith in one's good fortune and contentment in one's heart.

(Original, cont.)

5. **And all the souls that came out of the loins** (were born of) **of Jacob** (the supplanter) **were seventy** (10 x 7) (6) **souls: for Joseph** (increaser, he shall add) **was in Egypt** (in a state of material consciousness) **already.**
   6. **And Joseph** *(increaser, he shall add)* **died, and all his brethren, and all that generation.**
   7. **And the children** (ideas within the budding consciousness) **of Israel** (he who embarks on a search for God) **were fruitful, and increased abundantly, and multiplied, and waxed exceedingly mighty; and the land** (the untried consciousness) (7) **was filled with them** (with new thoughts, new spiritual ideas).
   8. **Now there arose up a new king** (a controlling mentality) **over Egypt** (the material consciousness), **which knew not** (was not aware of) **Joseph** (the increaser).
   9. **And he said unto his people** (8), **Behold, the people of the children of Israel** (souls ready to embark on a new journey) (9) **are more and mightier than we:**

FOOTNOTES:

(6). I suggest that the figure "seventy" is a composite of the number '10' which represents the executive power, and the number '7' which symbolizes individual completeness or fulfillment.

(7). The "land" is given in the dictionary as symbolizing the "bare ground", the *tabula rasa* upon which we are to cultivate our spiritual consciousness.

(8). The term: "his people" is a reference to the thoughts well anchored in the subconscious, i.e. the habitual, reliable, no matter how inept, concepts which we no longer question but take for granted.

(9). Depending on the context, "children" can symbolize the outcome of our deliberations, as well as souls ready to embark on a search for spiritual consciousness, or even the next step towards spiritual understanding.

(Application, cont.)

5. And all these attributes that are born of the desire for growth have the power to strive for fulfillment since the ability to expand the consciousness is already inherent in the material mentality.

6. That which motivated and increased all previous abilities, with all its attributes and all its achievements is now terminated.

7. And (in its place) new ideas born in the heart which embarks on the search for God are so fruitful, they multiply so abundantly, that they become exceedingly powerful; and the fresh mind, the innocent consciousness is filled with new thoughts, new spiritual ideas.

8. Now there are aspects of the mentality controlling the physical awareness, which do not seem aware of this new desire for growth.

9. And such a mind-set rebels against new concepts which prove more powerful than the old, established ways. This mind-set seems to cry out:

(Original, cont.)

10. **Come on, let us deal wisely with them; lest they** (the new ideas) **multiply, and it come to pass, that, when there falleth out any war, they join also unto our enemies** (10) (thoughts contrary to our convictions), **and fight against us, and so get them up out of the land** (the untried consciousness).

11. **Therefore they did set over them taskmasters to afflict them with their burdens. And they build for Pharaoh treasure cities, Pithom** (narrow way) **and Raamses** (sun).

12. **But the more they afflicted them, the more they multiplied and grew. And they were grieved because of the children of Israel.**

13. **And the Egyptians** (the concepts which bind us to a material consciousness) **made the children of Israel to serve with rigour:**

14. **And they** (those old concepts) **made their lives bitter with hard bondage** (powerful attachment), **in mortar, and in brick, and in all manner of service in the field: all their service, wherein they made them serve, was with rigour.**

FOOTNOTES:

(10). While "enemies" symbolize all negative thoughts, fears, doubts etc, in this case the symbol is used from the point of view of the negative consciousness.

(Application, cont.)

10. "Come, let us deal wisely with these new ideas; lest they multiply and in times of decision they unite against our ways, and side against us thus taking over our dominion."

11. Thus the old concepts set in our minds create all manner of difficulties, create real or imaginary problems. They reinforce themselves in their treasured states of consciousness from the most restrictive to the most powerful.

12. Yet the greater our attachment to the old habits, the more the new ideas seem to grow and multiply. The old ways are fighting a loosing battle against the new.

13. But our old beliefs in concepts reliant on the material consciousness fight hard to retain control of our minds:

14. They enslave us to the old transient and inferior ideas, and hold us back in all manner of our daily lives: they come up in all our daily activities, in whatever we do, they assault our resolve with vigor.

Explanatory Notes and Some Comments

The left-hand column copies the original text from the Holy Bible, King James Version. The bold letters were used to accentuate the original text, while words in the parentheses abbreviate the information that can be found in the Dictionary of Biblical Symbolism.

I cannot emphasize too strongly, that my sole concern was not for the *literal* accuracy of the interpretation, but for unraveling of the symbolic meaning behind original text. As stated before, in the days of Moses not many people would have been likely to be able to read. In order to convey his message, Moses must have spoken his thoughts in such a manner as to plant the seed of understanding in the minds of the greatest number of people.

The right hand column is my suggested application of the Dictionary in a manner that eliminates allegories. In other words, it endeavors to illustrate what Moses might have actually been saying, had he lived closer to our times, and had his followers enjoyed a reasonable command of the English language.

The above is no more than an *example* of how the Dictionary could be used. It is my contention, that there must be as many interpretations of the original text as there are people in the world. I have no doubt that other students will, in due course, provide us with vastly superior applications of the Dictionary. Until they do however, we must all cope on our own.

Good luck!

The Fourth Book of Moses:
NUMBERS
Chapter 13:1-16

(Original text in bold)

1. And the LORD (the I AM consciousness)(1) **spake unto Moses** (drawer out)(2), **saying,**

2. Send thou men (specific thoughts) **that they may search the land** (unchartered consciousness) **of Canaan** (low region), **which I give unto the children of Israel** (they who search for God): **of every tribe** (inborn traits) **of their fathers** (past) **shall ye send a man, every one a ruler** (capable of controlling his thoughts) **among them.**

3. And Moses by the commandment of the LORD sent them from the wilderness (mental void) **of Paran** (cavernous): **all those men were heads** (intellects) **of the children** (resulting from) **of Israel** (those who search for God).

4. And these were their names (3): **of the tribe of Reuben** (behold a son)(4), **Shammua** (famous) **the son (5) of Zaccur** (well remembered, mindful).

5. Of the tribe of Simeon (a hearing, harkening), **Shaphat** (judge) **the son of Hori** (free noble; cave dweller) **the son of Jephunneh** (appearing; for whom it is prepared).

FOOTNOTES:

(1). The LORD is regarded as the Indwelling Presence of God, nowadays variously translated as the I AM, the Christ Consciousness, the Divine Spark, the Indivisible Soul, the Higher Self, etc. I chose to translate the word as the Silent Voice, to assure that no reader will externalize the source of Moses' inspiration.

(2). Moses is treated here as a historical figure but, like Jesus, he can be regarded as an example of how to strive for oneness with our highest potential.

(3). As stated before, "names" in the Bible invariably indicate the nature, the characteristics and/or the quality of that which they "name".

(4). The "son" in *(behold a son)* is regarded here as symbolizing the birth of a new (his name shall be called Wonderful, Isa. 9:6) consciousness.

(5). Here the "sons" seem to symbolize the qualities resulting from efforts in the more immediate past as against the "tribe", which refers to the already established traits of character.

(Application)

1. And Moses heard the Silent Voice of the Divine within his soul urging him

2. —to gather his thoughts that they might search the unchartered regions of his awareness, the deepest levels of his mind, which were now given him (who persistently searches for God) to explore. And he knew, that every mental probe he would send must reflect a trait of character he developed over many years, over which he had achieved total conscious control.

3. And Moses (bid by the Silent Voice) emptied his mind even to the deep recesses of his cavernous subconscious: And every conscious thought was now a construct of pure intellect, begat of his desire to know God.

4. And these are the qualities which controlled his probing thoughts: of his long yearning for the new consciousness he reached out with great prominence derived from his previous knowledge and experience.

5. Of his ability to listen to his inner voice, he reached out with great discrimination born of often venturing into the mysterious subconscious.

(Original, cont.)

6. **Of the tribe of Judah** (praise, praise, let him be praised), **Caleb** (bold, impetuous) **the son of Jephunneh** (for whom it is prepared).

7. **Of the tribe of Issachar** (bearing hire, reward), **Igal** (deliverer, whom God will avenge), **the son of Joseph** (increaser, he shall add).

8. **Of the tribe of Ephraim** (doubly fruitful) **Oshea** (God saves, Jehovah is salvation) **the son of Nun** (continuation, fish).

9. **Of the tribe of Benjamin, Palti** (Jah delivers, deliverance of Jehovah) **the son of Raphu** (feared; healed).

10. **Of the tribe of Zebulun** (dwelling), **Gaddiel** (fortune sent from God) **the son of Sodi** (Jah determines, an acquaintance).

11. **Of the tribe of Joseph** (increaser, he shall add), **namely of the tribe of Manasseh** (causing forgetfulness) **Gaddi** (belonging to fortune, fortunate) **the son of Susi** (Jah is swift or rejoicing).

FOOTNOTES:

(6). While "land" would normally symbolize the opportunity to demonstrate the efficacy of one's consciousness, in this context, judging from all the preparations that Moses imposes upon himself, it is evident that he refers to very uncommon land. In fact, though he seems not quite aware of it as yet, he is venturing into the Promised Land.

(Application, cont.)

6. Of the inherent quality of ever-grateful heart, he prodded with boldness natural to one who is well prepared for this venture.

7. Of the ability to accept just reward for his efforts, he reached out in full knowledge of impending deliverance, derived from the constant striving to expand his consciousness,

8. And of being greatly fruitful in all his endeavors he knew that the Eternal One is his salvation and will assure his immortality.

9. And from being ever righteous and enjoying good fortune, his thoughts were confident regarding his deliverance, with confidence of one who once feared yet had been healed.

10. From ever abiding within the realm of his own consciousness his thoughts were confident of good fortune sent from God, as he already knew that the Eternal controls his destiny.

11. And of the inherent ability to multiply his blessings by his own efforts, now no longer needed, his thoughts were ever of good fortune, in natural consequence of the swiftness and rejoicing, which issues from the Eternal.

(Original, cont.)

12. **Of the tribe of Dan** (judge), **Ammiel** (my people is strong; God's people) **the son of Gemalli** (camel owner)

13. **Of the tribe of Asher** (happy), **Sethur** (secreted, hidden) **the son of Michael** (who is like God?).

14. **Of the tribe of Naphtali** (wrestling), **Nahbi** (Jah is protection, consolation; hidden) **the son of Vophsi** (rich; expansion?).

15. **Of the tribe of Gad** (the seer etc), **Geuel** (God is salvation; majesty of God) the **son of Machi** (smiting, afflicting, slaying).

16. **These are the names of the men which Moses sent to spy out the land** (6) (unchartered consciousness). **And Moses called Oshea** (God saves; Jehovah is salvation) **the son of Nun** (continuation; fish) **Jehoshua** (Jah saves; Jehovah is salvation).

(Application, cont.)

12. While of inherent vigilance and great discrimination, he sent out powerful thoughts, natural to one wielding great power over his physical body.

13. Yet masked by his inner contentment his thoughts remained ever hidden, forever inquiring into the mystery of the Divine.

14. And from his lifelong wrestling with test and tribulations, his thoughts learned of the Divine protection, the single source of the greatest riches.

15. While of great faith in his inherent good fortune, he learned that success is born of struggle and affliction

16. These are the qualities of thoughts with which Moses probed the unchartered oceans of his ever-expanding consciousness. And Moses named his Higher Self, the Son of the Eternal, the God of his salvation.

Explanatory Notes and Some Comments

In my edition of the King James Bible, this account is called "A first glimpse of the Promised Land."(1) The Promised Land is, of course, the new state of consciousness within which peace rules supreme (Jerusalem) and ultimately one achieves God realization (Zion). The above verses describe Moses' first attempts to venture into this unknown territory of pure consciousness.

His efforts are demonstrated by repetitive affirmations of positive thinking, by many references to his ever present good fortune, by his unshakable faith, as well as his reliance on his own past experience.(2) Perhaps the greatest lesson for us is that Moses had to master no less than twelve traits of his own character before he would even attempt to enter the Promised Land.

The number twelve (12 tribes), is of course symbolic. From the prodigious examples in the Bible, we learn that there are as many ways to heighten our awareness of the divine Spark within us, as there are people in the world. And it appears that, for most of us, there are indeed many more than twelve qualities to be mastered before making our attempt.

Paradoxically, if we do not struggle we don't get very far, and if we do... we must stop and enter the temple of peace which we have carefully built and maintained in our hearts. Sometimes it seem that we can do little more than maintain constant vigilance while we learn to listen to our Inner Voice.

He whose name symbolized Divine Love one said: "Be still; and know that I am God"(3).

FOOTNOTES

(1). The Holy Bible, (Tomas Nelson Inc.) Life in Bible Times, pg.28.
(2). Later Moses no longer needed "his own efforts" since he committed himself to the guidance of his Higher Self.
(3). Psalm 46:10

The Book of the Prophet
ISAIAH
Chapter 8:22 & 9:1-8.

[Isaiah's struggles for enlightenment]

(Original Text in bold)

22. And they (my thoughts) **shall look unto the earth** (physical consciousness); **and behold trouble and darkness** (inability to realize the presence of God), **dimness** (lack of direction, indecision) **of anguish; and they** (my thoughts) **shall be driven to darkness.**

Chapter 9

1. **Nevertheless the dimness shall not be such as was in her** (1) **vexation, when at the first he** (2) **lightly afflicted the land** (the original state of consciousness) **of Zebulun** (dwelling) **and the land of Naphtali** (m (3) **by the way of the sea** (mental awareness), **beyond Jordan** (flowing down)(4), **in Galilee** (the circle) **of the nations** (many thoughts).

2. **The people** (my thoughts) **that walked in darkness have seen a great light: they that dwell in the land of the shadow of death** (5) (physical consciousness), **upon them hath the light shined.**

FOOTNOTES

(1). "Her" being feminine refers to the soul or psyche. Regardless of the level of our conscious understanding, the soul is that which refers to the subconscious.

(2). Nowadays, we would spell he with a capital H. It refers to the I AM, or the Christ consciousness within us, which, though we are not aware of It, is ever trying to raise us to Its level

(3). This is soul again. In the Bible the soul incorporates the mental and emotional traits, as against the "man" or "body" which is our physical awareness.

(4). Jordan, being a river, signifies a purposeful change in consciousness. Crossing Jordan means making a new commitment.

(5). Since in Spirit, there is no death, "Shadow of death" obviously refers to the physical consciousness, The shadow, therefore, implies an illusion.

(Application)

22. I took stock of the results of my labors, of the world I have created; and all I could see were ever mounting problems, no hope for the future, lack of a sense of direction, the anguish of indecision; my thoughts turned to despair.

Chapter 9

1. Yet my consternation was not as great as when I had first sensed the whisper of the Silent Voice gently touching my budding awareness in which I was then struggling so greatly. Later, this same Divine Whisper made turbulent the ocean of my mind—though it was still before my commitment to the dictates of my new perception. It was in the days when I walked the treadmill of my established mind-set.

2. And even then I, who lived in such ignorance, had the first glimpse of the Divine Knowledge: and though my mind was still filled with the illusion of physical reality, it was then that I felt the first seeds of higher understanding.

(Original, cont.)

3. **Thou** (6) **hast multiplied the nation** (mental consciousness), **and not increased the joy: they** (the mental attributes) **joy** (7) **before thee according to the joy in harvest** (results), **and as men** (thoughts governing physical consciousness) **rejoice when they divide the spoil** (that which justifies their existence).

4. **For thou hast broken the yoke** (attachment) **of his** (8) **burden, and the staff** (support, that which one leans upon) **of his shoulder, the rod** (sceptre, the rod of power) **of his oppressor** (9), **as in the day of Midian** (contention; strife).

FOOTNOTES

(1). "Her" being feminine refers to the soul or psyche. Regardless of the level of our conscious understanding, the soul is that which refers to the subconscious.

(2). Nowadays, we would spell he with a capital H. It refers to the I AM, or the Christ consciousness within us, which, though we are not aware of It, is ever trying to raise us to Its level

(3). This is soul again. In the Bible the soul incorporates the mental and emotional traits, as against the "man" or "body" which is our physical awareness.

(4). Jordan, being a river, signifies a purposeful change in consciousness. Crossing Jordan means making a new commitment.

(5). Since in Spirit, there is no death, "Shadow of death" obviously refers to the physical consciousness, The shadow, therefore, implies an illusion.

(6). Isaiah addresses his own Higher Consciousness.

(7). The New King James Version offers, "rejoice"

(8). Here, "his" is a reference to Isaiah's lower states of consciousness.

(9). [1]The "oppressor" of our body is our mind and belief in limitations. Mind is said to be a magnificent instrument but a terrible master—hence "oppressor".

(Application cont.)

3. But although this awareness of my Higher Self has greatly increased my mental attributes, It does little to remove my discontent. My new intellect seems to rejoice as if lost in the vainglory of its new perceptions, even as my body rejoiced when sating its physical senses.

4. Yet this Power Within has broken my attachment to the things of my body (and all that it leaned on), as well as the domination of my intellect, which controlled my life even in the long days of my search and contention.

(Original, cont.)

5. **For every battle** (a struggle within one's consciousness) **of the warrior is with confused noise** (an abundance of thoughts), **and garments rolled in blood** (the influence of the ever-present spirit); **but this shall be with burning** (great cleansing) **and fuel of fire** (another metaphor for burning). (10)

6. **For unto us** (11) **a child** (new consciousness) **is born, unto us a son** (12) **is given: and the government** (princely power) **shall be upon his shoulder: and his name shall be called Wonderful, Counsellor, The mighty God, The everlasting Father, The Prince of Peace.**

7. **Of the increase of his government and peace there shall be no end, upon the throne of David** (Divine Love), **and upon his kingdom, to order it, and to establish it with judgment and with justice from henceforth even for ever. The zeal of the LORD of hosts** (Higher Consciousness control of the stream of thoughts) will perform this.

8. **The Lord** (the I AM, the Christ consciousness) **sent a word into Jacob** (awareness of one's spiritual nature), **and it hath lighted upon Israel** (conscious commitment to the search for Higher Awareness).

FOOTNOTES

(10). In biblical language, repeating a phrase, or a very similar idea, always serves to reinforce the notion or the statement.

(11). The use of plural "us" is of vital importance. It implies that we do not rise through various states of consciousness, dropping or destroying the lower nature. The plural form asserts that all the lower states must be raised, or redeemed in order to achieve enlightenment.

(12). The same literary form as above. Here the "child" and the "son" both refer to the birth of a Higher Consciousness, i.e. to the Divine Child, the Prince of Peace.

(Application cont.)

5. For in all my struggles I have been confused with divergent ideas, even as my consciousness sensed the Divine Presence; but now, I sense the moment of a great cleansing, a great freeing of the spirit within me.

6. For I feel the onset of a New Consciousness within me, a new awareness of the Divine Presence: and to It I submit control over the totality of being: for I know that Its nature is filled with a great wonder, that It will counsel me in all my endeavors, that there are no limits to Its awesome power, that It shall be the Source of my creation, while ever maintaining Divine Peace of my being.

7. And the serenity of Its presence shall grow in my heart forever, even as Its power emanates from the Divine Love of Its nature; and to Its judgment I submit my being. Such is the ardor of the Higher Consciousness.

8. When the Spirit first touched me, I became aware of Its presence. But it was only when I committed my whole being to the pursuit of God that the Christ Consciousness descended upon my awareness.

Explanatory Notes and Some Comments

A most beautiful passage. It is interesting to compare the way that Moses and Isaiah ventured into the reality of their Promised Land. There is, of course, only one Promised Land—but an infinite number of ways to experience Its Infinity.

The Promised Land, being a State of Consciousness, can only be realized at an individual level. It is said to be a reality wherein the micro and the macrocosm coexist in perfect harmony.

Apparently, no two people can share this Reality, yet all can experience It simultaneously. To Moses, It seems to encompass infinity, a state beyond the matrix time and space, immortality. Isaiah, on the other hand, is in awe of its Wonder, Its inherent beauty, and particularly Its Love and Serenity.

For me, it is a.... Oh, sorry!

What matters is: what is *your* Promised Land?

The Gospel according to
SAINT LUKE

Chapter 11:29 - 36

(Original text in bold)

29. And when the people were gathered thick together, he began to say, This is an evil (absence of the Divine Presence) **generation** (a mind-set): they (the thoughts) **seek a sign** (physical demonstration, fulfillment of prayers);(1) **and there shall no sign be given it, but the sign of Jonas** (dove) **the prophet.**

30. For as Jonas was a sign unto the Ninevites (stagnant condition), **so shall also the Son of man** (the redeemed human personality) **be to this generation.**

31. The queen of the south (soul capable of physical demonstration)(2) **shall rise up in the judgment with the men** (thoughts) **of this generation, and condemn them: for she** (soul) **came from the utmost parts of the earth** (physical consciousness)(3) **to hear the wisdom of Solomon** (peace);(4) **and, behold, a greater than Solomon is here.**

FOOTNOTES:

(1). Apparently we, in our physical or carnal consciousness are always bent on results. Here we appear to be taught that what matters is the process itself.

(2). Even as the 'king' controls our conscious thoughts, so the 'queen' symbolizes our soul, i.e. our subconscious and emotions.

(3). A lesson for the medical profession. We are taught that our subconscious mind is the direct result of our conscious 'thought' or 'idea' gathering. Thus we can only find peace in our subconscious (soul) by a *conscious* effort [as against drugs, chemicals and other forms of escapism etc.].

(4). Solomon symbolizes peace and Jonas a dove, which is a symbol of peace. Every modern psychiatrist will agree that whatever the method to improve one's mental or psychological condition, the first prerogative is to relax or set the patient at peace.

(Application)

29. And as the people gathered together [or, He gathered his thoughts and said:] Your whole mind-set shows total absence of Divine Inspiration: your thoughts seek fulfillment, an efficacy in their prayers, yet no prayers shall be answered; though you have achieved the semblance of an inner peace.

30. For as the omen of peace was given to those who remained set in their ways, so the redemption (1) of the human consciousness shall be the demonstration to sate your present state of mind.

31. The soul which fully realizes the Presence of God shall sit in judgment over your present notions and condemn your accumulated beliefs: for your soul has searched the farthest reaches of your conscious mind to find the wisdom of inner peace; and behold, a greater wisdom than that which gathers peace is yours to possess.

(Original cont.)

32. **The men** (thoughts) **of Nineve** (stagnant consciousness) **shall rise up in the judgment with this generation, and shall condemn it: for they repented** (5) **at the preaching of Jonas** (dove); **and, behold a greater than Jonas is here.**(6)

33. **No man, when he hath lighted a candle** (concentration, commitment), **putteth it in a secret place, neither under a bushel, but on a candlestick, that they** (thoughts) **which come in may see the light** (knowledge)(7)

34. **The light of the body** (physical consciousness or mind) **is the eye** (center of attention): **therefore when thine eye is single** (focal point), **thy whole body also is full of light** (knowledge); **but when thine eye is evil (no Presence of** God), **thy body also is full of darkness.**

35. **Take heed therefore that the light which is in thee be not darkness.**

36. **If thy whole body** (physical consciousness, conscious awareness) **therefore be full of light** (knowledge), **having no part dark, the whole** (8)(i.e. soul, total awareness) **shall be full of light, as when the bright shining of a candle** (total commitment) **doth give thee light** (knowledge).

FOOTNOTES:

(5). To repent can mean many things, including: 'to have another mind', to be penitent, comforted or eased.

(6). It is abundantly apparent that Jesus is addressing people who had once listened to the teaching of the prophet Jonas. The concept of reincarnation was a widely held belief in biblical times (as it is rapidly becoming today).

(7). In the biblical sense, there is no other than *spiritual* knowledge.

(8). The 'whole' means our conscious, subconscious and the emotional make-up of our personality, i.e. our soul (not to be confused with I AM). We are again taught that the vast memory banks of our subconscious mind are always being programmed by the input from our conscious awareness.

(Application cont.)

32. The thoughts of your stagnant consciousness shall rebel and sit in judgment upon your set ways and condemn them: for your mind has been eased at the prospect of peace, and behold, a greater consciousness than a promise of peace is now being offered.

33. No man, once committed to a search for the Divine Knowledge can become halfhearted, but he must place and keep his determination at the forefront of his attention so that all the new thoughts, concepts or ideas will be regarded in the light of this new commitment.

34. Physical consciousness (or conscious awareness) gathers Divine Knowledge by focusing its attention on a single objective: therefore when we become single minded in our pursuit, our whole mind becomes filled with new Understanding; however, if we attempt to focus our mind without commitment to the Highest Principles, we remain in abject ignorance.

35. Make sure then, that the knowledge you have gathered is not a knowledge of ignorance (selfish motivation).

36. If your whole consciousness is filled with Divine Wisdom, with neither doubts nor reservations, then your whole being will also be filled with this same Wisdom, even as your total commitment to a single purpose brought this great New Understanding to your conscious awareness.

FOOTNOTE

(1). Redemption invariably means rising to a spiritual level of consciousness, i.e. (inter alia) rejection of all limitations. Note that this does not as yet imply instant "re-programming of the subconscious" (which process is only explained in the Revelation of St. John); although the author (Luke) does claim that if our awareness is single-minded, the rest or "the whole" will follow.

Explanatory Notes and Some Comments

I sense a marked difference between the Old and the New Testament teaching. In the Old books the accent seems to be on specific traits of character, which must be overcome (redeemed) in order to progress any further.

One by one—an arduous process.

Here, the Teacher seems to assume that the kindergarten is over, and it is time to get down to serious business. The lesson is nothing less than an instruction on the method we must employ to achieve results (a demonstration of the efficacy our prayer). Although the physical results as such are not what really matter, we must still become proficient in the use of the method. We are told that inasmuch as the first step must be total relaxation, this is nevertheless only the first step. We are told that unless we concentrate all our efforts towards achieving greater knowledge, greater understanding, little will be achieved. And even then, we might venture into realm of knowledge that might prove of little use to us. Apparently, at all times we must remain vigilant

This is a pronounced stress on *knowledge*, as against *faith*, which is taken for granted. This is, perhaps, the greatest difference between the Gnostic and the so-called Orthodox interpretation of Biblical teaching. (1)

But what fascinates me the most is the statement that we can only "save our soul", or to put it in a more up to date language, to reprogram our subconscious mind and achieve a balanced personality, by a conscious effort. Apparently there are no shortcuts. No 'miracles.' Total concentration, total commitment, no wavering in our determination and, providing our goals are set very high and our motivation of the highest ethical order, we can do it.

What price the glory?

We know from Moses and Isaiah, that ultimately, the glory is Infinity, Immortality, Omnipotence, Peace beyond human understanding...

You decide...

Immortality??? (2)

FOOTNOTES

(1). See **INTRODUCTION**

(2) See *Key to Immortality* by the author. [Inhousepress 2003, Smashwords 2010]

REVELATION
of Saint John the Divine
Chapter 6:1-17

(Original text in bold)

1. **And I saw when the Lamb** (1) (the Christ Consciousness or Higher Self) **opened one of the seals** (that which guards access to the unconscious)(2) **and I heard, as it were the noise of thunder, one of the four beasts** (negative nature)(3) **saying, Come and see.**

2. **And I saw, and behold a white horse (spiritual nature): and he** (4) **(conscious awareness) that sat on him had a bow (effectiveness); and a crown (princely control) was given unto him** (5) **and he went forth conquering, and to conquer.** (6)

3. **And when he opened the second seal, I heard the second beast say, Come and see.**

FOOTNOTES:

(1). See **Dictionary** for a discussion of this concept.

(2). In early 1960's, Carl G. Jung postulated that the unconscious communicates with the conscious mind through symbols. According to him, the consciousness 'naturally' resists anything unconscious and/or unknown. The "seals" are, therefore, symbols or expressions of this superstitious fear of novelty know as misoneism. (For more information see *Man and his Symbols*, by Carl G. Jung (et all), © 1964 Aldus Books Ltd., London.

(3). The four beasts represent the fragmented traits of our character that place limitations on the four facets of human nature, i.e. the physical, emotional, mental and spiritual. We are not to reject all but the last, but to raise all of them to the spiritual level.

(4). In the Bible the conscious awareness is always symbolized as the masculine principle (Ra), while the soul is represented by the feminine principle (Is).

(5). There are many lessons in the Bible, which stipulate that conscious awareness is the only awareness that is, or must be, "in control". Ultimately it is this awareness that must be redeemed so that we enter the spiritual state of being in full consciousness. [This concept is the idea behind the victory over 'death', which anyway in only an illusion].

(6). In the Bible we are all treated as spiritual beings. As such, we are immortal, omnipotent, infinite, etc. What stops us from enjoying this condition of such being, are our false beliefs. And thus all that we must conquer is the recalcitrant belief in our limitations.

(Application)

1. I found it a profoundly traumatic experience when my Higher Self brought out the first of the mysteries hidden deep in my unconscious. And then, still from the point of view of my lower nature I felt compelled to witness the vision before me.

2. And I beheld the spiritual attributes of my human nature: and I realized that he who holds reins over this aspect of his being, has the power to vanquish all false images and to conquer all his limitations. (1)

3. And when still drawn by the curiosity entrenched in my lower nature, I was given to witness the second mystery:

(Original cont.)

4. And there went out another horse that was red (emotional nature): **and power was given to him that sat thereon** (7) **to take peace from the earth** (physical consciousness), **and that they** (rider and the horse) **should kill one another:** (8) **and there was given unto him a great sword** (effectiveness).

5. And when he had opened the third seal, I heard the third beast say, Come and see. And I beheld, and lo a black horse (intellect); **and he that sat on him had a pair of balances** (judgment, discrimination) **in his hand** (executive power).

6. And I heard a voice in the midst of the four beasts say, A measure of wheat for a penny and three measures of barley for a penny;(9) **and see thou hurt not the oil** (praise, thanksgiving) **and the wine** (secret knowledge).

7. And when he had opened the fourth seal, I heard the voice of the fourth beast say, Come and see.

FOOTNOTES:

(7). As above, note that each horse represents a different aspect of human nature, but "he who sits thereon" is always the conscious awareness. Thus we can never blame the horse, only the rider.

(8). It has been said that no war was ever started as a result of an intellectual deliberation, but invariably by a reaction to an emotional response. The same is true of the struggles within our consciousness.

(9). This price setting has no meaning other than an illustration of cool, mathematical, detached logic in contrast to the emotional response; it brings us neither joy nor progress on our spiritual path.

(Application cont.)

4. I saw the essence of my emotional body. And I sensed that he who allows his emotions to rule his awareness shall surely destroy the serenity of his being; and I saw that the conscious control and uncontrolled emotions cancel each other out with deadly efficiency.

5. And the third mystery showed me the function of my intellect. And even as I regarded the new vision, my awareness was flooded with the cold authority of judgment and discernment.

6. And all the four aspects of my nature mimicked the precision of the mental quibble with a cold karmic detachment devoid of any feeling; neither praising nor grateful, devoid of inspiration.

7. And as my Higher Self raised the fourth veil, my lower nature has again drawn me towards the unfolding vision.

(Original cont.)

8. **And I looked, and behold a pale horse** (physical consciousness): **and his name** (nature, character) **that sat on him was Death** (illusion)(10), **and Hell** (loss of awareness of the Presence of God) **followed with him. And Power was given unto them** (11) **over the fourth part of the earth** (human consciousness), **to kill with sword, and with hunger, and with death, and with the beasts** (the negative aspects) **of the earth** (the produce of human nature).

9. **And when he had opened the fifth seal, I saw under the altar** (raised consciousness) **the souls** (12)(psyche) **of them** (traits of character) **that were slain** (conquered, redeemed or overcome) **for the word of God** (Truth), **and for the testimony which they held;**

10. **And they** (those souls, or the redeemed attributes) **cried with a loud voice, saying How long, O Lord, holy and true, doest thou not judge and avenge** (vindicate) **our blood on them that dwell on the earth?**

11. **And white robes** (spiritual protection) **were given unto every one of them** (13) (that was redeemed); **and it was said unto them, that they should rest yet for a little season, until their fellow-servants also and their brethren, that should be killed** (conquered, overcome) **as they were, should be fulfilled.**

FOOTNOTES:

(10). See notes on "death" in the **Dictionary.**

(11). Note "them" which unifies the beast and the rider. At the 'physical' level the two are virtually one.

(12). While the author of the Revelation uses the more dramatic plural, I chose to continue my own interpretation as related to my own, individual state of consciousness. (We must never lose track of the fact that the Revelation is a dramatic presentation of the journey each soul must make on its way to God Realization).

(13). 'Testimony' in biblical sense refers to the tables of the Law, i.e. to the fulfillment of the Ten Commandments.

(Application cont.)

8. And there I beheld the quintessence of my carnal awareness. And I saw that this part of me subsists in a world of utter illusion—in total denial of the Higher Self within me. Yet this carnal awareness holds sway over one-quarter of my human consciousness. It has power to destroy higher impulses by starving my soul of the influx of Spirit. It has no notion of the Divine Presence within me, and it submits to the negative aspects of my lowest instincts.

9. And then my Higher Self unfolded to me the fifth mystery. And I had a vision of my soul being raised to a higher level of consciousness. I saw my soul, which for the sake of Truth and by fulfillment of the Law, had already overcome some aspects of its lower nature.

10. And in my vision the attributes that had overcome their limitations demanded, of the Higher Self, a vindication and judgment over those qualities, which were still part of my physical consciousness.

11. And the redeemed qualities were now part of my spiritual nature; and it became apparent, that the redeemed attributes are now indestructible, and as time in the spiritual realm is of no consequence, eventually all negative aspects of my lower nature shall be overcome even as I have vanquished some of my limitations already.

(Original cont.)

12. **And I beheld when he** (the Lamb) **had opened the sixth seal, and, lo, there was a great earthquake;**(14) **and the sun** (the conscious mind) **became black as sackcloth of hair, and the moon** (the subconscious) **became as blood;**

13. **And the stars**(15) **of heaven** (the acquired knowledge, the guiding lights) **fell unto the earth** (physical awareness)(16) **even as a fig tree casteth her untimely figs, when she is shaken of a mighty wind.**(17)

14. **And the heaven departed as a scroll when it is rolled together; and every mountain** (raised consciousness) **and island** (land, realized demonstration) **were moved out of their places.**

FOOTNOTES:

(14). It is apparent from this that the traits of character that we have already redeemed are 'stored', so to speak, in our subconscious, i.e. soul, while we continue our struggles on the spiritual paths. Apparently our positive (good) qualities become part of our spiritual consciousness, which is indestructible, though they appear to fade when next to the Divine (see later verses).

(15). An earthquake invariably symbolizes a traumatic experience.

(16). Stars are 'points of light', and light always symbolizes the source of (divine) knowledge. Thus the stars are symbolic of the knowledge we accept as the Truth, which is unchangeable, (though our understanding of It deepens with each step along our infinite journey).

(16). Here again we see that when the chips are down we are left to cope with our physical consciousness as best we can. [Until we redeem it, of course!]

(17). Although this phrase can be taken as a literary metaphor, we can also interpret the "untimely figs" as our improved, though still inadequate qualities, and the "great wind" as the powerful action of the Spirit.

(Application cont.)

12. And when my Higher Self revealed to me the sixth mystery I became greatly troubled; and my awareness has deserted me completely, even as my subconscious was flooded with the Divine Presence.

13. And what knowledge I have gathered now tumbled into oblivion, even as that which is incomplete tumbles when faced with the might of Spirit.

14. And in a single instant all semblance of peace had vanished; whatever I held as sacred, whatever experience I gathered I could no longer rely on.

(Original cont.)

15. **And the kings** (control) **of the earth** (conscious awareness)**, and the great men** (great concepts), **and the rich men**(18) (thoughts of prosperity or accomplishments)**, and the chief captains** (those in charge), **and the mighty men** (powerful ideas), **and every bondman** (attachment), **and every free man** (redeemed virtues) **hid themselves in the dens and in the rocks** (proven, or tested states of consciousness) **of the mountains** (raised state of awareness as in prayer)**;**

16. **And said to the mountains and rocks, Fall on us, and hide** (protect) **us from the face** (power of recognition, the omnipresence of God) **of him** (the Christ, the I AM, the Higher Self) **that sitteth on the throne, and from the wrath** (vindication, claiming) **of the Lamb** (the state of redeemed consciousness):

17. **For the great day of his wrath** (vindication) **is come; and who shall be able to stand?**

FOOTNOTES:

(18). Each "man" symbolizes a state of consciousness created by the thoughts, which the adjective accompanying each "man" indicates. We *all* are states of consciousness. When our thoughts are "happy", we are happy men, when sad, we are sad man, etc..

(Application cont.)

15. And I lost all control over the thoughts comprising my conscious being, all the great concepts, all thoughts of wondrous spiritual achievements, my aspirations of leadership, and the truly powerful ideas, and all my attachments and even what I thought were my virtues... all have retreated, forgotten, even as my mind withdrew into the tested grounds invoking the protection of prayer.

16. And then I tried to find solace in the stronghold of my contemplation. There I thought I could hide, away from having to face Him(1) that wields the Divine Power, from Him who lays claim to the sublime essence of my conscious being.

17. For the great day when He takes charge over my being is here. And I shall meet His ordinances in humble submission.

FOOTNOTES:

(1). As above, I employ the pronouns "Him" and "He" to symbolize the conscious as against the subconscious awareness which, in the Bible, is always symbolized by the pronoun "she".

Explanatory Notes and Some Comments

The Revelation of St. John is by far the most complex but also the most complete document in the Bible describing the nature of man and the process by which we can enter into the state of spiritual consciousness. It is presented as a drama wherein the reader is, on occasion, a dispassionate observer while in other scenes he is drawn into full participation as his own Higher Self unfolds the mysteries of the ultimate potential locked deep in the unconscious of the reader's mind.

This constantly shifting point of view adds to the complexity of the drama, as the mystery unfolds of the gradual metamorphosis of our lower nature, the beast within us, into a divine being.

It is significant that even in the "great day" when the Divine lays claim to our consciousness, we meet this moment of realization on bent knees, in awe of That which is within us. For "who can stand" when face to face with the Divine Presence?

John chooses to protect the information by a series of allegories. He wraps almost every word in a veil of symbolic meaning or at least a poetic expression. As the Bible has been translated into countless languages, the well-meaning thought recalcitrant theologians would have greatly "improved" on the meaning... had they understood it. The so-called "modern" editions of the Bible amply attest to this thesis. Yet I strongly suspect that the main reason behind John's apparent subterfuge had been to make the knowledge more universal.

The single chapter which I offer as an example how the Dictionary can be applied to even the most complex problems should be regarded as no more than my *personal* view of what may have been the author's intent. In no way do I suggest that my interpretation of the 'secret' knowledge is to be regarded as an authoritative statement on the 'Revelation'.

If fact, nothing would please me more than to receive abundant correspondence from people who found their *own* meaning, as their *own* Higher Self unfolds to them the mystery of the pilgrim's journey.

And what a magnificent journey it is!

Since we are all unique, individual expressions of the Divine Spark within us, it is only fitting that we should all be endowed with a unique interpretation.

"I am the way," once said a great Teacher.

So are You.

DICTIONARY
OF
BIBLICAL SYMBOLISM

A

Aaron enlightened, illumined; [light?] (possibly from Egyptian "great is the name")

Abaddon destruction, destroyer, a perishing; (Greek *Apollyon*)

Abagtha happy, prosperous, felix; given by fortune

Abana constant, permanent, perennial; stony

Abarim [c] passages, fords, ridges; regions beyond; {[c] identifies a city, town, place, court, house, tent or any 'condition' in which one would spend any length of time. All such 'conditions' invariably symbolize a STATE OF CONSCIOUSNESS. Occasionally the same word designates both, a person and a place}

Abda shortened from Obadiah: servant of Jah. [For the sake of brevity, throughout the Dictionary *Jah* is used as a contraction of *Jehovah* which is the English version of *Yahweh*] (see *Abi*)

Abdeel, Abdiel servant of God

Abdi servant of Jah, my servant

Abdon [c] service, servile

Abed-nego servant of light; servant or worshiper of Nego; [He symbolizes man's intellectual nature] (see *Shadrach*)

Abel 1. transitoriness, vanity, lamenting, mourner, mourning; [Symbolizes a halfhearted commitment to mind over matter; Abel represents the first *shepherd*, who in turn symbolizes *a keeper of thoughts*]

Abel [c] 2. fresh, grassy, meadow, stream, brook

Abel-beth-maachah [c] meadow of the house of Maachah

Abelmaim [c] meadow of the waters; (see *water*)

Abelmeholah [c] meadow of dancing

Abelmizraim [c] meadow of Egyptians; (see *Egypt*)

Abelshittim [c] meadow of acacias

Abi, Abia, Abiah Jah is father. [Jah is an abbreviation of Jehovah: literally *the existing one*. Since *The Existing One* is Spirit, the Bible ascribes the origin of all to Spirit].

Abialbon father of strength; (see *Abi*)

Abiasaph father of gathering, my father has gathered; (see *Abi*)

Abiathar father of superfluity

Abida father of knowledge, my father knows

Abidan father of judgment

Abiel, Abihail father of might, strength; God is my father

Abiezer father of help, my father is help

Abigail source [Jah is the father] of delight, exultation

Abihu He [*the Existing One*] is my father

Abihud father of honor; father of Judah

Abijah my father is Jah; father (i.e. worshiper) of Jah

Abijam father of light; father of the sea (or west); [also given as another spelling of *Abijah*] (see *light* and *sea*)

Abilene [c] a grassy place; a plain; [refers to the richness of the intellectual aspect of consciousness which is, nevertheless, below the spiritual realm]

Abimael my father is (El) God; (see *El*)

Abhimelech father of the king; my father is king; (see *king*)

Abinadab father of liberality; father of nobility

Abiner, Abner father of light; [*light* symbolizes the source of (generally higher or divine) knowledge].

Abinoam father of pleasantness, my father is pleasant

Abiram father of [elevation], loftiness. [He that raises consciousness]

Abishag father of error, i.e.: cause of wandering

Abishai father [source] of wealth; father of gift.

Abishalom father of peace; (see *Absalom*)

Abishua father of safety or welfare; [my father saves?]

Abishur father of oxen; father of the wall

Abital father of dew

Abitub father [source] of good

Abiud father of honor; (see *Abihud*)

Abner father of light; [literally: "my father is a lamp"] (see *Abiner*)

Abraham father of a multitude; [symbolizes the abundance of thoughts, spiritual ideas. *Ra* represents the masculine principle thus the executive state of mind, a rational faith. In the broadest sense Abraham, Isaac and Jacob (who became Israel) symbolize body, soul and spirit].

Abram father of height; the father is exalted; [The original name of Abraham. Abram symbolizes the spiritual *height* that leads him to become Abraham, the father of a multitude i.e.: of an abundance of thoughts and (spiritual) ideas].

Absalom father of peace; (see *Abishalom*)

Accad castle, fortress; [often a *fortress* or a *walled city* symbolize a 'closed' consciousness].

Accho [c] compressed; [a confined consciousness (limitation?)]

Aceldama portion of blood, a field of blood; (Piece of ground purchased by Judas with money he received for betraying Jesus).

Achan, Achar trouble; troubler

Achbor a mouse

Achim woes

Achish serpent-charmer; (see *serpent*)

Achor [c] trouble

Achsa, Achsah anklet; serpent-charmer

Achshaph [c] dedicated; enchantment

Achzib a winter brook, a lie; deceit.

action (of God) invariably symbolizes help, i.e. it

presupposes a positive attitude regarding all matters of divine origin.

Adadah [c] bordering; [festival?]

Adah pleasure; ornament

Adaiah pleasing to Jah; whom Jehovah adorns

Adam red earth, clay, of the ground; [symbolizes a state of consciousness which identifies itself with the physical body. N.B.: In the allegory of the Garden of Eden, Adam and Eve actually symbolize one person consisting of body and soul]. (see *Eve*)

Adamah [c] red earth, fortress; [the color red often symbolizes (uncontrolled) emotions].

Adar fire god; [the 12th month of the Jewish religious year, starting from the new moon of March].

Adar, Addar [c] height, honor

Adbeel languishing for God; [miracle of God?]

Addan, Addon [c] strong

Ader flock

Adiel ornament of God, God is an ornament

Adin, Adina, Adino ornament; slender; voluptuous; [different scholars offer one or more of the three meanings for all the three names]

Adithaim [c] two ways, or passages; twofold ornament

Adlai weary, lax; just

Admah [c] earthwork, fortress

Admatha God given; [untamed?]

Adna, Adnah pleasure, delight

Adonibezek lord of lightning

Adonijah Jah is my lord

Adonikam my lord is risen; [lord of enemies?]

Adoniram my lord is high, lord of height, my lord is exalted

Adonizedek lord of justice, my lord is righteous

Adoraim [c] double honor, [two chiefs?]

Adoram high honor; (contracted from *Adoniram*)

Adrammelech honor of the king; [magnificence of the

king? king of fire?]

Adriel honor of God; flock of God; God is my help

Adullam resting place; justice of the people

adultery the word is interchangeable with *infidelity* and *idolatry*. The biblical writers refer to the relationship between the masculine principle: the conscious mind (*Ra*), and the feminine principle: the soul (*Is*)

Adummim [c] red things, red places; the red [men?]

Æeneas praise, [praiseworthy?]

Ænon (natural) fountains, springs

Agag high, warlike; [a poetic name for *Amalek*]

Agar [Greek name for *Hagar*]

Agee fugitive

Agur gatherer, collector, assembler

Ahab uncle, (literally: father's brother)

Aharah after the brother

Aharhel after might; behind the breast-work; [anguish, feverish heat?]

Ahasai my holder, protector

Ahasbai blooming, shining; [refuge is in Jah?]

Ahasuerus king

Ahava stream

Ahaz he holds, possessor

Ahaziah Jah holds, possesses; whom Jah upholds

Ahban brotherly, brother of intelligence, brother is a builder; (see *brother*)

Aher one that is behind, following

Ahi my brother

Ahiah Jah is a brother, brother of Jah.

Ahiam a mother's brother; [brother of the father?]

Ahian brother of day, brotherly

Ahiezer helping brother, brother of help

Ahihud 1. brother of honor, my brother is majesty; 2. brother of mystery, my brother is a riddle

Ahijah (same as *Ahiah*)

Ahikam my brother rises or has risen, [brother of the

enemy?]

Ahilud a brother born, brother of one born; a child's brother

Ahimaaz powerful brother; brother of anger, wrath

Ahiman brother of man; brother of a gift

Ahimelech brother of the king, my brother is king; (see *king*)

Ahimoth brother of death, my brother is death

Ahinadab brother of liberality; brother of a nobleman

Ahinoam pleasant brother, brother of grace, my brother is pleasantness

Ahio his brother, brotherly; [little brother?]

Ahira brother of evil, of a wicked man; my brother is Ra (the Egyptian sun-god]

Ahiram exalted brother; brother of a tall man

Ahisamach supporting brother, brother of aid

Ahishahar brother of the dawn, my brother is the dawn

Ahishar brother of song (or of the singer); [bother is upright?]

Ahithophel foolish brother, brother of impiety

Ahitub a good brother, brother of goodness

Ahlab [c] fruitful place; fertility

Ahlai Jah is staying; the brother of my God; [sweet?]

Ahoah a brother's reed

Aholah (Oholah) [c] her own tent; [A symbolic name for Samaria and the ten tribes. In a wider sense, before there were cities, or villages, there had been *tents*. Since *city* invariably symbolizes a state of consciousness, presumably tent in still earlier times served to symbolize the same as the city].

Aholiab a father's tent

Aholibah [c] my tent (is) in her; [A symbolic name for Judah and Jerusalem. "Her" is obviously the "soul" and "tent" refers to the state of consciousness the soul is enjoying].

Aholibamah tent of the high place; [describes a person

(called Judith in Genesis 26:34) of a high state of consciousness]

Ahumai heated by Jah; brother of [i.e. dweller near] water

Ahuzam a holding fast; their possession

Ahuzzath holding fast, possession, grasp

Ai [c] the heap, a heap of ruins, a heap of stones

Aiah, Ajah a falcon, vulture or hawk

Aiath a heap, a ruin, ruins. [The feminine form of *Ai*]

Aija (same as preceding)

Aijalon [c] place of gazelles

Aijeleth shahar hind of the morning, dawn; [title of Psalm 22].

Ain [c] a (natural) fountain, a spring or an eye

Ajalon (see *Aijalon*)

Akan (or **Jakan**) acute, twisted

Akkub lain in wait; a guard; [insidious?]

Akrabbim curves or scorpions; scorpions

Alameth covering, concealment; [youthful vigor?]

Alammelech [c] the king's oak, royal oak

Alamoth soprano or treble, [a term derived from *Almah*: "a virgin"]

Alexander helper of man; defending men

Aliah (Alvah) sublimity, height

Alian (Alvan) sublime; tall

Alleluia praise ye the Lord, praise Jah

Allon [c] an oak, strong tree

Allon-bachuth [c] oak of weeping, strong tree of weeping

Almodad the agitator; agitated; incommensurate; immeasurable; [extension?]

Almon [c] hidden, hiding place; way-mark

Almon-diblathaim [c] waymark of the two fig cakes; hiding of the two cakes; hiding of troubles; [The 39th encampment of Israel after leaving Egypt, the 28th from Sinai]

Aloth [c] ascents, steeps; [yielding milk?] (*Be'aloth* = mistress)

Alpha [first letter of Greek alphabet. The title of Christ, "the Beginning" as in *Alpha and Omega*: the beginning and the end, meaning completeness]. (see *El*)

Alpheus, Alphæus leader, chief; successor

altar symbolizes raised consciousness; [it is a state of awareness wherein we make contact with our higher nature].

Al-taschith destroy (or corrupt) not, do not destroy; [in titles of Psalms]

Alush [c] wild place; [the 9th encampment of Israel on the way from Sin to Sinai].

Alvah (see *Aliah*)

Alvan (see *Alian*)

Amad [c] station; people of duration, [eternal people?] [It could symbolize thoughts which linger, thus a stagnant state of consciousness]

Amal labor, laboring, sorrow, trouble

Amalek warlike, dweller in the vale

Amam [c] gathering place

Amana [c] permanent, fixed

Amariah Jah has said (or has spoken)

Amasa burden-bearer; burden; (also see: *Amashai*)

Amasai Jah has borne; burden bearer, burdensome

Amashai carrying spoil

Amasiah Jah has borne, burden of Jah; Jah has strength

Amaziah Jah has strengths, Jah strengthens

Aminadab my people is willing; people of the prince; the kinsman is generous; [whichever translation one chooses, it is evident that Aminadab symbolizes thoughts and/or concepts of the highest quality, i.e.: of divine inspiration]. (see *people*)

Amittai truthful, true

Ammah [c?] an aqueduct

Ammi my people; [symbolize *spiritual ideas* of Israel, i.e.: *thoughts* of one engaged on a conscious search for

God].

Ammiel my people is strong; people of God; [thus *Ammiel* symbolizes divine inspiration]

Ammihud my people is honorable; my kinsman is majesty; (see *people*)

Ammihur my people is noble; [symbolizes noble ideas, aspirations]

Amminadab my people is willing; people of the prince, (see *Aminadab*)

Amminadib my people is liberal or generous; [or same as preceding]

Ammishaddai my people is mighty, people of the Almighty; [symb. mighty concepts of divine origin]

Ammizabad my people is endowed; people of the giver [i.e. Jehovah, therefore spiritual ideas]

Ammon a fellow countryman or kinsman; [symb. shared concepts or ideas]

Amnon tutelage, up-bringing; faithful, trustworthy

Amok deep; capable

Amon workman; faithful

Amorite mountaineer; [a mountaineer could symbolize a person who relies heavily on prayer or on religious practices].

Amos burden-bearer; burden

Amoz strong

Amphipolis [c] about the city, surrounded city; (named from the river Strymon flowing around the city)

Amplias enlarged, (short form of *Ampliatus*)

Ampliatus (see preceding)

Amram exalted people, people of the highest (i.e. God); (see *people*)

Amzi my strength, strong

Anab [c] a hill; a grape, place fertile in grapes

Anah answering

Anaharath [c] narrow way; [Anaharath is a city in *Issahar* meaning *bearing hire, reward.* Compare Matt.7:14:

"...narrow is the way, which leadeth into life"]

Anaiah Jah answers, Jah has answered

Anak giant, long-necked

Anakim giants; [Descendants of Arba: the strength of Baal personifying the male principle devoid of the female component, i.e.: executive power without soul].

Anamim rock-men

Anammelech the king's rock; image of the king; [Pertains to idol worship among the Sepharvaim which was transplanted to the cities of Israel]

Anan he beclouds; a cloud

Anani my cloud [i.e.: protector]. *Anani* is shorter form of *Ananiah*: *whom Jehovah covers*. [Symb. protection of the Higher Self]

Ananiah Jah is a cloud [i.e.: protector]. (see preceding).

Ananias Jah is gracious; (Greek form of *Hananiah*)

Anath answer; an answer to prayer; [symbolizes a demonstration of a raised consciousness].

Anathema anything placed or set up in a temple of a god, set apart or separated, consecrated or devoted; something accursed

Anathoth answers; answers to prayer; (see *Anath*)

Andrew manly

Andronicus conqueror, victorious man

Anem [c] double fountain, springs

Aner sprout, waterfall; [a young man?]

Anethothite A native of Anathoth; [possibly: he who obtains answers to prayers].

angel 1. mighty; 2. messenger, agent. [*Angel* is used as a symbol for a messenger, positive or negative, from the divine or from men, and is applied to a wide variety of entities, including prophets, priests, ministers, as well as to the pillar of cloud and fire, to the (pestilential) winds, disembodied spirits, etc. Such messengers may or may not be personified, depending on the individual making contact with his or her inner Self]

A

angels (elohim) God, a god, judge; the meaning is
    dependent on the context (see *elohim*)
Aniam lamentation of the people
Anim [c] fountains
animals (in the ark) *clean* animals symbolize the positive
    instincts, attributes, faculties; unclean animals
    symbolize the human traits yet to be redeemed. (see
    beast)
Anna grace
Annas grace of Jah; [Greek form of *Hananiah*]
antichrist symbolizes the opposite of Christ consciousness,
    i.e.: consciousness steeped in materiality and
    limitation, denying the Spirit within].
Antipas father's image; [an abbreviation of *Antipater*, the
    father of Herod the Great]
Antothijah answers of Jah; [prayers answered by Jah?]
Antothite belonging to Anathoth; (see above)
Anub strong or high; [bound together?]
Aphek [c] fortress; strength; [i.e.
a state of consciousness both safe and powerful or, if
    implying a *walled city*, it could symbolize a
    consciousness not open to new ideas]
Aphekah [c] (see preceding)
Aphiah striving; scull; fontanel
Aphik [c] fortress (see *Aphek*)
Aphrah [c] hamlet; dust
Aphses the dispersed, dispersion
Apollonia [c] place of Apollo; [Apollo, or Phoebus
    Apollo, the Greek god of light, music, poetry, pastoral
    pursuits, prophecy and healing thus, a state of
    consciousness personifying some or all of such
    qualities].
Apollos a destroyer
Apollyon destruction, destroyer; one that exterminates;
    (Greek translation of *Abaddon*)
apostle means: one sent forth, thus a messenger, an

85

ambassador.

Appaim face, presence; the nostrils; little nose

Aquila an eagle; [an eagle symbolizes the conquered (re-deemed) emotional nature]

Ar [c] city; [any town or city symbolizes a state of consciousness]

Ara strong; [lion?]

Arab [c] a court; ambush

Arabah a plain, wilderness; (see *plain, wilderness*)

Arabia wilderness; darkened; toward the west; unproductive; sterile; (see *wilderness*)

Arabian [those who live in the wilderness]

Arad fugitive; wild ass

Arah traveler, wayfarer; wandering

Aram high, exalted; height

Aram-naharaim *Aram:* of two rivers; (Psalm 60, title)

Aran wild mountain goat; firmness

Ararat [c] creation, Holy Land

Araunah Jah is firm; a strong one; a hero; [calf?]

Arba, Arbah [c] strength of Baal; giant; strength; (see *Anakim*) [The city of Arba symbolizes the consciousness of Ball].

Arbite native of the wilderness

Archangel the chief messenger; (see *Michael*)

Archelaus people's chief, prince

Archi [c] the long

Archippus chief groom, the master of the horse

Archite the long; [the native of *Erech*]

Arcturus group, crowd; [the constellation commonly called the Great Bear].

Ard sprout, decent; humpbacked; [fugitive?]

Ardon descendant; fugitive; [humpbacked?]

Areli valiant, heroic

Areopagus Mars' Hill; (Mars, the Greek *Ares* was a god of war)

Aretas pleasing; virtue; power; purity

Argob [c] strong; a rocky district; mound

Aridai delight of the (god) Hari? strong; worthy; [Persian: *Haridaias*]

Arieh lion of Jah; lion

Ariel lion of God; (see *Lion of God*)

Arimathea a height; high place; [i.e. a raised consciousness, normally through prayer].

Arioch lion-like

Aristarchus the best ruler

Aristobulus the best counselor

ark (the) symbolizes a (powerful) mental sanctuary which we should build when sensing formidable difficulties looming on the horizon.

Arkite fugitive

Armageddon hill (or height) of Megiddo (i.e.: *place of God*). [Symbolizes the attainment of Christ consciousness, thus: the final victory over one's limitations. Traditionally it is recognized as the scene of a great spiritual battle].

Armenia [Greek form of Ararat: (*creation, holy place*)].

Armoni of the palace; belonging to a palace; a palace man

Arnan strong; active

Arnon [c] rushing stream; swift; [Stream, like river, always symbolizes a directional movement, thus a (purposeful) change in consciousness]

Arod descent, posterity; wild ass; humpbacked

Arodi my posterity; (see preceding)

Aroer [c] enclosed; juniper; ruins; desolation; barren; naked;

Arpad, Arphad [c] a couch, resting place, support

Artaxerxes great king; honored king; mighty warrior;

Artemas whole, sound; gift of wholeness; [contracted from *Artemidoros*, meaning a gift of Artemis, a goddess of fertility and childbirth].

Aruboth [c] courts; windows

Arumah [c] height, elevated, lofty

Arvad [c] refuge; wandering

Arza firm; earth; [delight?]

Asa physician, healer; [or a contraction form *Asaia*, meaning: Jah has healed].

Asahel God is doer, whom God made, God has made; [Symbolizes the Higher Self as the causative element in our consciousness]. (see *El*)

Asahiah, Asaiah Jah is doer, Jah has made; (see *Jah, Jehovah*)

Asaph collector, gatherer

Asareel God is joined; whom God has bound

Asarelah Jah is joined; [right before God?]

Asenath dedicated to Neit; she, who is of Neith, [spelt either way: a goddess of the Egyptians?]

Aser happy; [Gr. form of *Asher*]

Ashan [c] smoke

Ashbea man of Baal; I conjure; plenty (see *Baal*)

Ashbel man of Baal; reproof of God; (possessor of) a long upper lip; [blame?]

Ashchenaz (see *Ashkenaz*)

Ashdod [c] fortress, castle, a strong place

Ashdoth pisgah springs or slopes of Pisgah; [atop the spurs and ravines of Pisgah is Mount Nebo: *a lofty place*].

Asher happy; fortunate

Asherah the goddess *Ashtoreth*

Ashima heaven; [an idol worshiped by the people of Hamath: *a walled city*, which symbolizes a consciousness closed to the action of spirit].

Ashkelon [c] holm-oak; migration; sojourn; stranger;

Ashkenaz hidden fire; fire that spreads; (A son of Gomer, grandson of Japheth...)

Ashnah [c] fortification; strong

Ashpenaz horse's nose; (The prince of eunuchs under *Nebuchandnezzar*) (see *eunuch*)

Ashriel (see *Asriel*)

Ashtaroth wife; riches; abundance; good fortune; stars; (also) **Ashtoreth, Astaroth**. [An idol of the Philistines (et al.) worshipped by Israel and Solomon. Presumably wife = woman, i.e. *human soul* (psyche) as against the Lord (*El*)

Ashteroth-karnaim [c] Ashte-roth of the two horns; [As ten horns symbolize great power, two horns sound rather limited; possibly, they refer to having physical and mental, or emotional and mental, or male and female, but not spiritual power].

Ashtoreth [c] a wife; she who enriches; [also an idol of the Philistines, Phoenicians, and Zidonians, worshipped by Israel soon after the death of Joshua as well as by Solomon]

Ashur freeman; [national god of Assyrians, king of gods etc.]

Ashvath maid, wrought

Asia [in ancient times, the territory included Bithynia, Cappadocia, Caria, Cilicia, Galatia, Lydia, Lycaonia and Isauria, Lycia, Mysia, Pamphylia, Paphlagonia, Phrygia, Pisidia, and Pontus].

Asiel God is doer; created by God; God is my maker

Askelon (see *Ashkelon*)

Asnah dweller in the thorn-bush; bramble

Assnapper Asnap the great; Assur has formed a son

Aspatha horse-given

Asriel God is joined; the prohibition of God

Asshur, Assur level plain; straightforward; harmonious; gracious; happy; the gracious One; hero. [Greek = Assyria]

Asshurim mighty ones

Assir prisoner; captive

Assos approaching; (a sea port, also called *Appolonia*)

Assyria plain, level [Hebrew = Asshur]

Astaroth see *Ashtaroth*

asuppim gatherings, [not a proper name, but left

untranslated; it denotes granaries, storehouses, collections]

Asyncritus incomparable

Atad [c] thorn bush; buckthorn

Atarah a crown, ornament, diadem

Ataroth, Atroth [c] crowns, wreaths

Ater bound, lame, crooked, crippled

Athach [c] lodging, inn; lodging place

Athaiah Jah is helper; [whom Jah made? Jah is superior?]

Athaliah Jah is strong; Jah is exalted; whom Jah has afflicted

Athens (c) [The most celebrated city in ancient Greece, originally built on the Acropolis by Cecrop, an Egyptian. Name changed to Athens from the worship of Athenæ (Minerva), the goddess of wisdom, patron of arts, of peace and war, ruler of storms. N.B.: she was a virgin goddess, having sprung from the forehead (intellect) of Zeus].

Athlai Jah is strong, exalted; (probably shortened from *Athaliah*)

Atroth crowns; [Atroth-shophan means the *wreath of Shophan*] (see *Ataroth*)

Attai seasonable, opportune, timely

Attalia (a seaport) that increases; [Named after the royal founder of the city: Attalus].

Augustus sacred, kingly, venerable, majestic (A emperor of Rome, thus a title and meaning assigned by Rome)

Ava [c] region; (a district near Babylon)

Aven [c] vanity, nothingness, wickedness [Egyptian city of *On* or *Heliopolis*. As all 'cities' it symbolizes as state of consciousness]

avenge (to) a biblical expression meaning to vindicate (see *vengeance*)

Avim, Avites [c] villagers; ruins; [1. A tribe destroyed before Moses; 2. a city in Benjamin; 3. a tribe transported to Samaria].

Avith [c] hut, village: [capital of Hadad: *mighty*, the son of Isaac who sold his birthright to Jacob]. (see *Isaac, Jacob*)

Azal [c] declivity, slope; root of mountain

Azaliah [c] Jah is noble; whom Jah has reserved

Azaniah Jah is hearer; Jah has given ear

Azarael, Azareel God is helper; whom God helps**Azariah** Jah is keeper; whom Jah aids

Azaz strong; [the Bible normally refers to spiritual strength].

Azaziah Jah is strong; whom Jah strengthened

Azbuk pardon

Azekah [c] breach; dug over; a hacked-up (place)

Azel noble

Azem [c] fortress; strength, bone

Azgad worship, supplication; strong in fortune; [messenger?]

Aziel God is might, whom God strengthens, my strength is God

Aziza strong

Azmaveth counsel or strength of death **Azmon** [c] fortress; robust

Aznoth-tabor ears or (twin) peaks of Tabor. [Tabor = *mountain height,* thus symbolizing prayer or raised consciousness].

Azor helper

Azotus [c] fortress, castle; [Greek form of *Ashdod*] (see *fortress, walled city*)

Azriel God is my helper; help of God

Azrikam my help has risen, help against an enemy

Azubah forsaken

Azur (same as *Azor*)

Azzah [c] fortress; strong, fortified; (see *fortress*)

Azzan sharp; strong

Azzur helper or helped (same as *Azor*)

B

Baal, Baalim master, possessor, lord, owner, husband
[Chief male deity of the Phœnicians and Canaanites;
(Ashtoreth was their chief female deity); Also given as
fertility-god].**Baalah** [c] mistress, possessor
Baalath [c] belonging to Baal; mistress.
Baalath-beer [c] lady of the well; having a well; mistress
of the well
Baal-berith lord of a covenant; [an idol worshiped in
Israel]
Baale [plural of Baal]
Baal-gad [c] lord of fortune; Gad is Baal; (see *Gad*)
Baal-hamon [c] lord of the multitude; place of a multitude
Baal-hanan the lord is gracious; lord of benignity
Baal-hazor [c] lord of Hazor (meaning: *enclosed*); having
a village
Baal-hermon [c] lord of Hernon (meaning: *prominent,
rugged*); place of Hermon.
Baali my lord; [a title rejected by God in favor of Ishi (*my
husband*)]
Baalim lords
Baalis (contraction of Ben-alis) son of exultation, of joy; in
exultation, joy; [nothing to do with Baal]
Baal-meon [c] lord of habitation; place of habitation
Baal-peor lord of the opening. [An idol of Moab which
Israel was enticed to worship; (Moab =*water of a
father*)]
Baal-perazim [c] lord of breaches, place of breaches, lord
of breaking forth
Baal-shalisha [c] lord of Shalisha, lord or place of Shalisha
(see *Shalisha*)
Baal-tamar [c] lord of the palm, place of palm trees
Baal-zebub lord of the fly, (flies) [An idol of the

Philistines, (philistia = *migration*)]

Baal-zephon lord of the north, lord of Typhon, place of Zephon; [sephon = *dark, wintry, north*] (see *north*)

Baana, Baanah son of grief, patient, son of oppression

Baara a wood, daughter of the fresh; foolish

Baaseiah Jah is bold; work of Jah

Baasha boldness; [wicked?]

Babel [c] *Babil* or *Babilani* in Babylonian = a gate of god; in Hebrew *Babal* = to confuse

Babylon [c] confusion; in Babylonian *Babilani* = gate of the gods, (or gate of Bel, which is another form of *Baal*, the Greek form of the Hebrew *Babel*). [It symbolizes mental limitation, acceptance of negative attitudes as reality]. (*see Sheshach*).

Babylonians sons of Babel. [This can symbolize both, the people who accept negative attitudes as reality, as well as the negative thoughts themselves, i.e. the product of such a state of consciousness].

Baca [c] weeping; [Hebrew *bakah* = to weep]

Bachrite belonging to Becher: (*beker* = a young male camel, thus possibly: *youth, first born*)

Baharumite belonging to young men; (see *Barhumite*)

Bahurim [c] (*town of*) young men; low grounds

Bajith [c] house; [or temple of the gods of Moab as opposed to 'high places'].

Bakbakkar diligent searcher

Bakbuk waste, hollow; a bottle

Bakbukiah wasted by Jah; emptying [i.e. wasting] of Jah; bottle of Jah

Balaam a pilgrim or lord of the people; [or from Hebrew *bil'am*; possibly: glutton, devourer, or from *bala*: to swallow]

Balac, Balak void, empty, waster, devastator; to make empty

Baladan having power; (God) has given a son

Balah [c] withered, old

Balak (see *Balac*)
Bamah [c] high place, elevation; [any place where Israel
    offers a sacrifice is a *high place*. It is important to
    differentiate to whom the sacrifice is being offered.
    Bamah designates places in which Israel offered
    sacrifices to idols].
Bamoth [c] high places; (see preceding)
Bamoth-baal [c] high places of Baal
Bani posterity; built, builder; [if a contraction of *Benaiah*
    = Jah is builder].
Barabbas father's son; son of Abba, i.e. father
Barachel blessed of God; whom God blessed
Barachiah, Barachias blessed of Jah, whom Jah blesses,
    Jah is blessed
Barak lightning, thunderbolt
Barhumite belonging to young man; an inhabitant of
    Bahurim
Bariah fugitive
Bar-jesus son of Jeshua; [otherwise called *Elymas* = a
    wise man, or a sorcerer who turns out to be a false
    prophet].
Bar-jona son of Johanan; [in Greek son of Jona (or John),
    which was Simon Peter's surname].
Barkos party-coloured; son of (the Edomite god) Qaus; a
    painter
Barnabas son of consolation, or of exhortation, or of
    encouragement
Barsabas son of Saba; [*seba* = man?]
Bartholomew son of Tolmai (= great?)
Bartimæus son of Timœus [Hebrew: *Timai*]
Baruch blessed
Barzilai strong, iron, of iron, the iron one
Bashan [c] the fruitful, fertile, soft rich soil, stoneless plain
Bashemath, Basmath fra-grant, sweet smelling, perfume
Bath-rabbim daughter of many, daughter of a multitude
    [the name of a gate of Heshbon] (see *gate*)

Bath-sheba daughter of an oath
Bath-shua daughter of prosperity
battle symbolizes a mental struggle with the belief in one's limitations.
Bavai wisher
Bazlith, Bazluth asking; [a making naked?]
Bealiah Jah is lord; whom Jah rules
Bealoth [c] ladies, mistresses
beast (the) symbolizes our carnal, negative nature – those traits of character which assert and uphold (false) limitations. [The *beast* is a symbol evocative of Carl G. Jung's analytical psychology, which promulgates a theory that even a *modern* man can be "powerless in the face of the autonomous emotions erupting from the unconscious" which, according to Jung, controls his instinctual nature.] {*Man and his Symbols*, edited by Carl G. Jung, Part four: *Symbolism in the visual Arts*, by Aniela Jaffé, pg. 264.}
(four) beasts In the Book of Revelations, the beasts symbolize the negative aspects of the fourfold human nature: a calf (or ox or bull) represents the body or the physical plane, the beast with the "face of a man" represents the intellect, a flying eagle: the (conquered) emotional nature, and the lion stands for the spiritual body. [In Rev.4:6-9, the Greek word *zoon* (translated as beast) is literally "a living thing" or "a living being". Either way it is symbolic of a lower nature, which must be raised to a higher level of consciousness. (see *horses*)
Bebai fatherly; child
Becher youth, first born; a
young camel
Bechorath first birth; offspring of the first birth, first born
Bedad son of Adad; separation, part, alone
Bedan son of judgment; [son of Dan?]
Bedeiah servant of Jah, (shortened from *Obadiah*)

Beeliada the lord knows; whom Baal has known

Beelzebub lord of the fly; [*zbl B'l* = prince Ball. If, however, we accept the Dead Sea scrolls designation of *zbl* for one of the 7 heavens of the Hebrew tradition, Beelzebub would symbolize a state of consciousness where "the evil one abides"] (see *Baal-zebub*) {Gleaned from the *Seventh-Day Adventist Bible Dictionary* by Siegfried H. Horn Ph.D. ©1960, 1979 by the Review and Herald Publishing Assoc. referred to hereinafter as SDA}

Beer [c] a well (artificial); [wells symbolize (inexhaustible) sources of spiritual inspiration. Even as water symbolizes human psyche, so wells are the sources of spiritual ideas, thus implying a receptive state of consciousness].

Beera, Beerah expounder; declarer; explainer; well; fountain.

Beer-elim well of heroes, trees, terebinths or chiefs

Beeri expounder; man of the well, belonging to a well.

Beer-lahairoi well of the living one that holds me; well of the vision [of God] to the living; well of the Living One who sees me.

Beeroth [c] wells; (plural of Beer)

Beer-sheba [c] well of the oath; [*sheba* = oath, abundance or seven].

Beesh-terah [c] house of Ashterach; (see *Ashtaroth*)

Bel lord; [Babylonian name for Baal]

Bela, Belah consumption, destruction, confusion, devoured

Belaite belonging to Bela

Belial worthless, reckless, lawless, wicked; [the children bear the fruit of their origin, thus a "son of a Belial" = a worthless or wicked person]

Belshazzar the lord's leader; Bel protects (the king)

Belteshazzar the lord's leader; preserve his (i.e. the king's) life

Ben son, intelligent

Benaiah Jah is intelligent whom Jah has built, Jah is builder

Ben-ammi son of my people; son of my own kinsman

Bene-berak sons of lightning

Bene-jaakan sons of intelligence

Ben-hadad son of (the god) Hadad; [= son of mighty]

Ben-hail strong, valiant; son of the host; a brave man

Ben-hanan very gracious; son of one who is gracious

Beninu posterity; our son

Benjamin son of the right hand (i.e. fortunate); son of the south. [His mother, Rachel, has named him Benoni, (son of my sorrow). Later his father changed his name to Benjamin, or Benyamin]. "The son of the *south* " would symbolize a successful demonstration, i.e. an answer to the prayers.

Beno his son

Benoni son of my sorrow; (see *Benjamin*)

Ben-zoheth corpulent, strong

Beon lord or house of On; (or contraction of *Baal-meon*)

Beor shepherd; burning

Bera gift

Berachah blessing

Berachiah, Berechiah Jah is blessing, whom Jah has blessed

Beraiah Jah is maker, whom Jah created, Jah has created

Berechiah (see above)

Bered [c] seed place; hail

Beri expounder; man of the well

Beriah unfortunate; excellent

Berith a covenant; [an idol *Baal-berith* was worshipped in Shechem]

Bernice Victoria, (Greek *bernike* = victorious)

Berodach-baladan bold; Berodach (same as *Merodach*) has given a son

Berothah [c] food; wells; [cypresses?]

Berothai [c] cypresses of Jah; my wells

Besai treading down; [sword? or victory?]

Besodeiah given in trust in Jah; in the secret (intimacy) of Jah

Besor cool brook, refreshing, (see *river*)

Betah [c] confidence, trust, security

Beten [c] height; a hollow

Beth-araba [c] place (or house) of passage {*Beth*, meaning a house or a place, always symbolizes a state of consciousness.}

Beth-anath [c] house of echo, echo, house (or temple) of a Canaanite goddess Anath

Beth-anoth [c] (same as preceding)

Bethany [c] house of dates or figs, house of the poor, of poverty

Beth-arabah [c] house of the desert or wilderness (see *desert*)

Beth-aram [c] house or place of the height; (see *Beth-haran*)

Beth-arbel [c] house of God's court; house of the ambush of God

Beth-aven [c] house of iniquity, of wickedness and/or vanity [i.e. of idols]

Beth-azmaveth [c] house of Azmaveth; house of strength; [*azmabeth* = death is strong]

Beth-baal-meon [c] house of Baal-meon; [i.e.: house of *lord of habitation*]

Beth-barah [c] house of the ford, fording place

Beth-birei [c] house of my creation, place of the city

Beth-car [c] house of lamb, place (or house) of pasture

Beth-dagon house or temple of (the god) Dagon; [= ho. of *fish*]

Beth-diblathaim [c] house of the two [circles] cakes [of figs].

Beth-el [c] house or temple of God; (see *El*)

Bethelite symbolizes one who abides in a high state of consciousness

Beth-emek [c] house of the valley. [As a *mountain* symbolizes prayer, i.e.: raised con-sciousness, one can assume a *valley* to imply the opposite, particularly since the text refers to the north].

Bether separation; [perhaps a poetical form of *Bithron*]

Beth-esda [c] house of mercy, of olives and/or of grace {*Beth*, meaning a house or a place, always symbolizes a state of consciousness.}

Beth-ezel [c] place of declivity; a place nearby; [house of firmness?]

Beth-gader [c] walled place, house of a wall; (see *walled city*)

Beth-gamul [c] place of the camel; house of the weaned; house of rewards

Beth-haccerem [c] place (or house) of the vineyard

Beth-haggan [c] house of the garden

Beth-haran [c] high or strong place

Beth-hoglah [c] place of magpies; house of the partridge

Beth-horon [c] place (or house) of the hollow; house of (the god) Horon; [A god worshiped also in Egypt and Ugirat as *Bt Hrn*] {Gleaned from SDA}

Beth-jeshimoth [c] place of desolations, of the deserts, wastes

Beth-lebaoth [c] place (or house) of lionesses; (see *lion*)

Beth-lehem [c] place of food; house of bread. (see *bread*)

Beth-maachah [c] place (or house) of oppression

Beth-marcaboth [c] place (or house) of chariots

Beth-meon [c] place (or house) of habitation; (see *Beth-baal-meon*)

Beth-nimrah [c] (place of) flowing water; (house of) sweet or clear water; [note: flowing (moving) water always symbolizes a change in or a changing consciousness].

Beth-palet (-phelet) [c] house of escape

Beth-pazzez [c] place of destruction; house of dispersion, shattering

Beth-peor [c] house of the opening; temple of (the god) Peor, (i.e. of *opening*)

Beth-phage [c] house of (unripe) figs

Beth-rapha [c] place (or house) of fear

Beth-rehob [c] house of a wide street; roomy place; (see *Rehob*)

Beth-saida [c] place of nets; house of fishing; (the native city of Andrew, Peter and Philip. In another city of same name 5000 had been fed).

Beth-shan [c] house of security; house of rest.

Beth-shean [c] (as preceding)

Beth-shemesh [c] house of the sun

Beth-shittah [c] place (or house) of acacias

Beth-tappuah [c] place of fruit trees; house of apples

Bethuel [c] dweller in God; house of God; [a man's name and a place in both cases it refers to a high state of consciousness]

Bethul [c] dweller in God; (same as preceding)

Beth-zur [c] place of rock; house of the rock {*Beth*, meaning a house or a place, always symbolizes a state of Consciousness.}

Betonim [c] heights; pistachio nuts

Beulah married

Bezai shining, high

Bezaleel God is protection; in the shadow of El: [i.e. of Higher Self] (see *El*)

Bezek [c] breach; [lightning?]

Bezer [c] strong; fortress; ore of precious metal

Bichri youth, first born; young

Bidkar servant of Kar; Son of Deker [?] (a captain who served *Jehu*)

Bigtha given by fortune

Bigthan, Bigthana given by God

Bigvai happy, or of the people

Bildad lord Adad, son of contention; [the son of (the god) Adad?]

Bileam [c] place of conquest; [Hebrew *ibleam* = people's canal]

Bilgah bursting forth, i.e. firstborn; cheerfulness, brightness

Bilgai (same as preceding)

Bilhah tender; modesty

Bilhan tender; modest

Bimhal circumcised

Binea wanderer

Binnui 'familyship'; a building, built

Birsha thick, strong, ugly

Birzavith olive well, well of an olive tree; [wounds?]

Bishlam in peace

Bithiah daughter of Jah, worshipper

Bithron [c] broken or divided place; a gorge [a district in *Arabah*: plain, wilderness]

Bizjothjah [c] place of Jah's olives; contempt of Jah

Biztha eunuch

Blastus a bud, a shoot, a sprout

Blood symbolizes the Essence, the Spirit, Divine Presence of Life Itself. What blood is to the physical body, Spirit is to the body of the (awakened) soul. (see *bread*)

Boanerges sons of rage, soon angry; sons of thunder

Boaz fleetness, strength

Boaz (pillar) symbolizes Logos, the power of the Creative Word, i.e. that which gives man power to change his condition through the recognition of the One Universal Principle (God).

Bocheru youth, first born

Bochim [c] the weepers

body symbolizes physical consciousness, our conscious awareness, or the state of mind of which our (physical) body is a reflection [In a broader sense, the "Body" also symbolizes the individualization of Soul. In more developed states of consciousness, such as the Body of Christ, It symbolizes the conscious awareness of I AM, the Higher Self].

Bohan stumpy; thumb

bond men symbolizes attachments as well as debts or obligations

bond woman soul constrained by its perceived limitations (see *woman*)

Booz (Greek form of *Boaz*)

Boscath [c] stony, elevated ground; (see *Bozkaz*)

Bosor the father of Baalam; (Greek and Aramaic form of *Beor*)**bottomless pit** symbolizes the very deepest, the most inaccessible level of our subconscious mind.

Bozez [c] height, shining

Bozkath [c] height, swelling

Bozrah [c] sheepfold, fortification, restraint, fortress

bread often symbolizes the Divine substance; it is that which sustains the "body".

breath symbolizes that which gives life, which enlivens, i.e. Spirit; (see *wind*)

brother need not define or even imply a family relationship, but rather expresses an nearness or affinity.

buildings often symbolize the human soul, i.e. aspects of our consciousness, which we are to build up from the state of 'wilderness' to the temple in the 'city of Jerusalem'.

Bukki mouth of Jah; 'proved of God'; wasting

Bukkiah mouth of Jah; wasting from Jah; 'proved of God'

Bul rain-god; rain; [the 8th month in Jewish religious year starting from the first new moon of October or November]

Bunah understanding; prudence

Bunni my understanding; built

burning symbolizes the cleansing action of Spirit. (see *fire and brimstone*)

Buz contempt

Buzi contemned of Jah; descended from Buz

C

Cabbon [c] circle, hamlet, hilly; cake

Cabul [c] dry, sandy, circle [displeasing?]

Cæsar [In the New Testament, the Roman emperor. He symbolizes the material consciousness that not be destroyed but redeemed]

Cæsarea [c] [a seaport on the great road from Tyre (*rock*) to Egypt].

Cæsarea Philippi [c] [the most northerly point of Christ's journeys]

Caiaphas depression; [the high priest of the Jews who presided at the trial of Jesus]

Cain acquisition, possession, one acquired; (commonly: worker in metal, smith) [symbolizes material, i.e. physical consciousness. Epitomizes fighting error with error].

Cainan, Kenan acquisition, possessor, worker in metal

Calah [c] firm; [in Sumerian etymology could mean a "holy gate"]

Calcol sustaining; [the perfect one?]

Caleb bold, impetuous; a dog

Caleb-ephratah [c] Caleb the fruitful

called (the) symbolize everyone of us; [the **chosen** symbolize those who choose God, the faithful are those who trust in the Truth].

Calneh [c] fort of Ana or Anu; complete concentration; centralized ambition; [Ana or Anu was among the chief objects of Babylonian worship]

Calno (same as preceding)

Calvary a scull; [adopted from Latin *Calvaria* i.e. *bare skull*. In Greek the name is *Kranion* which is the Chaldean translation of the word *Golgotha* meaning *scull*].

calves of our lips means: fruit of our lips, i.e. symbolize praise to God.

Camon [c] standing place; abounding in stalks

Cana [c] place of reeds

Canaan [c] low, flat; low region; red purple

Canaanite a zealot; [this translation would reinforce the last of the preceding: *red purple*, which carries the symbolic meaning of roused emotions]

Candace [a tile, not the name of the queen-mother of a Nubian or Ethiopian dynasty].

candle a lit candle is a source of light, thus of knowledge. More particularly, it is a focal point upon which we can fixate our attention. Thus a lit candle symbolizes not only the ability to concentrate but also a single-minded commitment to a search for Truth.

Canneh set up, distinguished

Capernaum [c] village of Nahum; city of consolation; shelter of comfort. In Matt.9:1 it is called: "his own city."

Caphtor [c] cup; covered and surrounded, changed; [the principle seat of the Philistines]

Caphtorim changed, converted [people of Caphtor]

Cappadocia fine horses

Carcas severe; vulture

Carchemish [c] citadel or fortress or quay of (the god) Chemosh: (=*fire, hearth*) [an idol of the Moabites and Ammonites, but not identical with Molech].

Careah (Kareah) bald head; bald

Carmel [c] fruitful place, garden or orchard; [The meanings of the words offered as well as the fact that Carmel is a *mountain* serve to symbolize a raised state

C

of consciousness].

Carmi fruitful, noble; a vine dresser

carnal mind symbolizes the physical or animal consciousness: that which recognizes the phenomenal universe as the sole reality.

Carpus fruit; harvest

Carshena lean, slender; black; spoiler; distinguished

Casiphia [c] white, shining; pale; place of the silversmith

Casluhim expiatory trials; fogiveness of sins; hopes of life; [In Psalm 68:31 this word is rendered *princes*].

Castor (& **Pollux**) [sons of Jupiter by Leda, recognized by sailors as their tutelary divinities: (stars in constellation of Gemini, or *Twins*)

Cauda see *Clauda*

Caves symbolize that which is buried in our subconscious; (see *pit*)

Cedron torrent; dark or dirty; [*Nahal Kidron* is the dark or black torrent which flows down the ravine below the East wall of Jerusalem].

Cenchrea millet, small pulse; [eastern harbour of Corinth]

Cephas rock; stone; [Surname given to Simon Peter]

Chalcol, Calcol sustaining; [the perfect one?]

Chaldea [c] savant; magi; astroloter; [The southern portion of Babylonia]

Chaldeans [Inhabitants of Shinar with Babylon as capital. They are classed with astronomers and magicians].

Chaldees (as preceding)

chamber is where consciousness resides; (see the *secret place*)

Chanaan [c] (see Canaan)

Charashim [c] craftsmen; [*Ge-harashim* = valley of craftsmen}

Charchemish (see *Carchemish*)

Charran (see Haran: *strong, enlightened*)

Chebar joining; the great one; [a river in Babylonia, thus symbolizing a change or an opportunity for a change in consciousness]

Chedorlaomer sheaf band; [or a servant of (the goddess) Laqamar, or of (god) Lagamar, depending on the source.]

Chelal completeness, completion, perfection

Chelluh robust; destroyed

Chelub boldness; bird trap; basket

Chelubai (see Caleb)

Chemarims servants, priests; persons dressed in black attire; [used only for idolatrous priests].

Chemosh fire, hearth; subduer; [An idol of Moabites] (see *Carshemish*)

Chenaanah flat, low; [from Canaan? If so, consider emotional connotations]

Chenani Jah, creator; Jah has established; (probably same as *Chenaniah*)

Chenaniah whom Jah supports, Jah has established

Chephar-haammonai [c] village of the Ammonites

Chephirah [c] village, hamlet: [of the Hivates: *villagers, 'midlanders'*. Hivites were peaceful, commercially inclined people]

Cheran union; harp, string instrument;

Cherethites executioners, mercenaries

Cherith trench, brook, gorge**cherub** one grasped, held fast; [blessing? strong? 'Cherub' in Hebrew is *kerub*; in Akkadian *Karâbu* = to bless, whereas *Karubu* = intercessor]

cherubim those grasped, held fast; (plural of *Cherub*)

Chesalon [c] fortress; hope

Chesed wisdom; astrologer, magi; [conqueror? Hebrew *Ke'sed* = a Chaldean]

Chesil [c] fleshy, carnal; flat; a fool; ungodly

Chesulloth [c] fatness, the loins; confidences; (the town may have derived its name from being situated on the slope of a mountain)

Chezib deceitful, false, treacherous

Chidon destruction, a javelin; [thrust?]

child symbolizes the new, spiritual Self or the Spiritual Idea. 'A woman with child' symbolizes a condition wherein a soul having conquered its (present) limitations is about to give birth to a new Self, a new Spiritual Idea, approaching oneness with the Christ within. [Note: 'giving birth' to a new Spiritual Idea is an ongoing process]. (also see below)

children symbolize the results or produce of our mental processes, i.e. thoughts, ideas, which in time become manifest in the phenomenal (physical) world.

children of Israel symbolise people ready to embark on a conscious search for God.

Chileab perfected by the father; like unto the father.

Chilion pining; wasting away

Chilmad inclosed; surrrounded; closed. (A region between Assyria and Arabia, trading with Tyre)

Chimham longing, pining

Chinnereth [c] circuit (around the sea of Galilee); a lyre, harp

Chinnoroth (as preceding) [plural of *Chinnereth*]

Chisleu Orion, Mars, hunter; hopeful, confident; [name of the 9th month November or December]

Chislon strong; confidence, hope

Chisloth tabor [c] loins of Tabor; flanks of Tabor; [Tabor means *mountain height,* i.e. prayer or raised consciousness].

Chittim (Kittim) terrible, giants

Chiun image; [*Kiyun* or *Kaywan* was the Hebrew name for the planet *Saturn*, perhaps the same as the idol *Ramphan*, which Israel worshiped in the wilderness. In Roman religion, Saturn was the god of harvest].

Chloe tender growth, green herb**Chorashan** [c] smoking furnace

Chorazin [c] place of proclamations

chosen (people) symbolize thoughts selected as attesting to the Presence of God. The word also symbolizes souls who choose God over negative, material reality. (see *called*)

Chozeba [c] deceitful; deceiver

Christ anointed; (Hebrew: *Mashîach*, Greek: *Messiah*). [Symbolizes the indwelling, redeeming Power, the Presence of God. Also referred to as the Christ Consciousness, the I AM, the Cosmic Consciousness, the Higher Self].

Chub [name of people in alliance with Egypt (*material-ity*) in the time of Nebuchadnezzar]

Chun [c] founding; establishment

church (Greek *ekklesia*) means: that which is called out.

Cinneroth (see *Chinnereth*)

Cilicia cruel, treacherous

circle is an ancient symbol of completeness, i.e. of the Higher Self which, the Bible teaches, is not a lord over the "lower" aspects of nature, but is that which (eventually) incorporates all the elements within Itself in a state of perfect balance. The circle is the basis of the religious symbol expressed by the *mandala* (symbolizing the union of the cosmos and the divine powers), and later by the *yantra*, such as the *Star of David*, which consists of 2 inter-locking triangles which symbolize the union of the opposites. (see *El*)

city [c] invariably symbolizes a state of consciousness. Various cities in the Bible illustrate different states of consciousness.

city of God Symbolizes a raised state of consciousness, e.g. *Jerusalem*. (see *House of God*)

cloud often symbolizes divine protection.

Clauda brocken, lame

Colhozeh wholly a seer, every one that sees, he sees all

Conaniah Jah is founding; (same as *Cononiah*)

Coniah, Cononiah Jah is creating, whom Jah has set up, Jah has established

Core baldness; (Greek form of *Korah*)
Coz nimble; thorn
Cozbi deceitful; the luxuriant one
crescens growing, 'moonlettes', little moons; [possibly crescent-shaped pendants worn as jewelry]
Cretans carnal, fleshy
Crete (as above)
Crispus curled
crown [symbolizes control, power over oneself; ability to live consciously rather than as a reaction to one's conditioning (the subconscious)].
cumi arise, rise up; [a feminine imperative, thus *Talitha cumi* (Mark 5:41) = "Maiden, arise"].
Cush, black, blackened, butned, Ethopia; Cyrus the sun; throne
Cushan blackness
Cushan-richathaim blackness of injustice, iniquity; wickedness, lies
Cushi black (same as *Cush*)
Cuth or **Cuthah** separating; fear
Cyprus [c] measure of corn; (fairness?)
Cyrene [c] wall
Cyrus the sun, throne; [the founder of the Persian empire, who conquered Babylon, and assisted the Jews]

D

Dabareh [c] pasture (see *Daberath*)
Dabbasheth [c] height; hump of a camel
Daberath pasture, leading to pastaure; arranged in order
Dagon fish; [the national god of the Philistines. Its form had the face and hands of a man, and the tail of a fish; In Hebrew *dagan* means grain, thus a "grain god?"] (see *fish*)

Dalaiah Jah is deliverer, whom Jah hath delivered, Jah has drawn (me).

Dalmanutha [c] bucket; overhanging branch{gleamed from MBD (Unity)}

Dalphon dropping; otherwise dropping; [proud? sleepless? (A Persian or Akkadian word)].

Damaris a young wife, a heifer

Damascene belonging to Damascus

Damascus [c] activity; alertness (regarding trade or possessions); sack of blood; [A city of Syria in a plain of great fertility]

Dan [also c] judge

Daniel God is Judge, God's judge, God is my judge; [-*el* = Higher Self].

Dan-jaan [c] Dan is playing the pipe; Dan of the woods; [woodland?]

Dannah [c] low, depressed; fortress

Dara bearer, holder; pearl of wisdom; (probably contracted from *Darda*)

Darda [a pearl of wisdom?] (see preceding)

Darius one who conserves; one who restrains; upholding the good; {from MBD}

darkness symbolizes the absence of spiritual light (i.e.: knowledge), or one's inability to realize the Presence (i.e.: Omnipresence) of God.

Darkon bearer, carrier; [scatterer?]

Dathan fount, spring [in Akkadian *datnu* = strong]

David beloved; [the name *David* symbolizes Divine Love]

dead (the) *The dead* symbolize those who, as yet, have no awareness of their Divine heritage. ["The pre Jacob stage"]

dead bodies symbolize ideas, thoughts or concepts which appear to have been overcome or 'lost' in the ongoing battle with our negative nature (the *beast*). [In fact 'redeemed' qualities become part of our spiritual consciousness and thus are indestructible].

death Symbolizes: 1. the loss of awareness of the Divine Presence; 2. a change in the state of consciousness. 3. illusion. [It is important to remember that in the biblical sense we are spiritual beings, thus immortal. To the Spirit, death is an illusion, or a termination of one state of consciousness only to enter another. [Compare: 1 Corinthians 15:31: "I die daily"] In Luke 20:35-36 "...neither can they die any more", refers to reincarnation, a concept widely accepted during biblical times. In Revelation 3:12 "...and he shall go no more out" refers to the same idea. The Bible seems to stipulate that once a certain state of consciousness has been reached the need for reincarnation as a perfecting instrument in no longer necessary.

Debir speaker; a recess; sanctuary; [original name: *Kiriath-sepher* = house of the book].

Deborah bee, wasp

Decapolis [c] ten cities [collectively]

Dedan [also c] low

Dedanim [descendants of Raamah: *trembling*]

Dehavites villagers

Dekar lance bearer; piercing, a piercing tool

Delaiah Jah is deliverer, whom Jah has freed, Jah has drawn me

Delilah languishing; delicate; coquette, flirt

Demas popular

Demeritus [belonging to Demeter, the Greek goddess of corn, harvest and fruitfulness]

(demonstration) (see *sign*)

Derbe [c] harsh

desert a general term symbolizing one's inability to realize the Presence of God, without defining the difficulty causing such a condition; (see *wilderness*)

Deuel God is knowing, knowledge of God; [same as

D

Reuel?]

Deuteronomy a repetition or recapitulation of the law

devil (Heb. *sair*): hairy one, kid, goat; (Heb. *shed*): spoiler, destroyer; (Gr. daimonion): daimon, demon, shade; (Gr. daimon): a difiled spirit; (Gr. diablos): accuser, calumniator; [All the above are translated as devil. The devil is always symbolizes the product of the mind]

diamond symbolizes the unchanging principle.

Diana moon goddess, virgin goddess; [The Greek divinity Artemis. As the goddess of the moon, she might symbolize control over the subconscious]

Diblaim double embrace; two cakes, double fig cake

Diblath circle; fig cake; [see Riblah: *fertility*?]

Dibon [c] river course; wasting; [This is a halting place of the Israelites after leaving Egypt. A *river course* would suggest a place where a *change* in consciousness occurred, or must occur in order to progress any further in the spiritual development].

Dibon-gad [c] wasting of Gad; (or same as the preceding)

Dibri on the pasture born; eloquent

Didymus a twin

die, dying (to die) see *death*

Diklah palm grove, a palm tree, date palm, place of palms

Dilean [c] gourd; cucumber-field; protrusion

Dimnah [c] dung, dunghill

Dimness like darkness, symbolizes the absence of spiritual light i.e.: knowledge; more particularly, dimness implies a state of indecision, a loss of direction.

Dimon [c] river bed; wasting; dung

Dimonah [c] (as above)

Dinah judged or avenged; vindi-cated

Dinaites jedgment

Dinhabah [c] place of plundering robbers' den. (The royal city of Bela, son of Beor, king of Edom, a Horite)

Dionysius [a follower of Dionysus or Bacchus, the god of wine. Wine often symbolizes spiritual knowldedge]

Diotrephes nourished by Zeus

Dishan leaping; antelope, gazelle; fertile

Dishon (same as preceding)

Dizahab [c] golden, of gold, lord of gold, a place abounding in gold

Dodai beloved of Jah; loving

Dodanim (or **Rodanim**) civilized, pleasing

Dodavah Jah is loving, love of Jah, beloved of Jah

Dodo loving (see *Dodai*)

Doeg fearful, timid, anxious

door (s) symbolizes a *change* in consciousness resulting in *new understanding;* (see *gates*) [Doors are between rooms which symbolize states of consciousness. In the biblical idiom any place where one abides for any length of time invari-ably symbolizes a state of consciousness].

Dophkah [c] cattle driving; [the 8th station of Israel on the way to Sinai]

Dor [c] circle; dwelling

Dorcas doe, gazelle

Dothan [c] double feast; two wells or cisterns. [Indeed such a "city" would be close to a mountain (near Mt. Bilboa)]

dove symbolizes a sense or a promise of peace.

dragons symbolize complexes anchored deep in the subconscious.

Drusilla watered by dew

dry land (Genesis) symbolizes thoughts materialized, i.e.: appearing in the objective or physical reality. In other words, the end product of the creative process.

Dumah [also c] silence, dumb, a tomb

Dura [c] circle; [in Akkadian = wall]

dwelling symbolizes a state of consciousness wherein one is apt to spend, or has spent, a length of time, thus it may represent a "stagnant" condition.

E

eagle symbolizes the redeemed (conquered) emotional
  nature. [*Scorpio* in the *Zodiac* is sometimes
  represented by a snake (or other reptile) or by an eagle.

earth symbolizes the physical consciousness i.e. our
  conscious awareness, as well as the sum total of the
  physical or phenomenal manifestations. (Also see
  world)

earthquake symbolizes a traumatic experience, a loss of
  conscious control. (also see *thunder*)

east symbolizes hope or spiritual regeneration as well as
  inspiration and the Presence of God, [Hebrew
  habitually faced *east* when giving directions, thus *east*
  was before or in front, *west*: behind or at the back,
  south was (on) the right hand, and the *north* : on the
  left].

Ebal [also c] bare; stipped of all covering; barren; stony.

Ebed servant, slave

Ebed-melech servant of the king

Ebenezer [c] stone of the help

Eber, (**Heber**) the other side, the region beyond; a shoot

Ebiasaph the father of gathering; (same as *Abiasaph*)

Ebronah bank, beach, coast [passage?] [The 30th station
  of Israelites in the wilderness. Each station
  symbolizes an attainment or an experience of new state
  of consciousness].

Ecclesiastes preacher; speaker before the conregation;
  [Attributed to Solomon, written in his old age. Its
  symbolism implies the benefits and the fruit of
  experience]

Ed witness

Edar, Eder [c] flock; troop; herd.

Eden [c] delight; pleasantness; [The initial state or

condition from which human consciousness began to evolve. One can infer from the precepts of psychology postulated by Dr.Jung that the initial "condition of delight" is a state of consciousness wholly dependant on instinct. One immersed in such a condition cannot "contemplate" a desire that is not part of his or her nature, and thus is capable of neither good nor evil. Hence the condition of "pleasantness"] {For further reading see *Man and his Symbols* by Dr. Carl Jung and his colleagues, mentioned before.}

Eder flock (same as *Edar*)

Edom [c] red; [while noting that his name is said to derive from the *red pottage*, the colour red symbolizes *emotion*]

Edrei [c] sown land; strong

Eglah calf; heifer

Eglaim [c] double spring, two pools, two drops

Eglon [c] circle; young bull; [An Amorite city in the "low country"]

Egypt black, the black (land); [In Hebrew Mitsraim meaning: shut in, distress. While some scholars suggest the etymology meaning "mansion of the Ka (god) of Ptah", in the Bible Egypt symbolizes materiality and physical limitation].

Ehi unity; shortened from Ahiram: [*brother of a tall man*]

Ehud strong, joined together, united

Eker offspring, root; [or the same as *Achar*]

Ekron [c] naturalization; eradication; [deep rooted?]

El- found in compound names only. *El* is the divine principle in human consciousness, i.e. our Higher Self. It is that through which we are able to contact the Existing One, i.e. *Jehovah* (*Yahweh*). As such it symbolizes the union of the Father (masculine) and Mother (feminine) principles making the Third, thus *El* represents the *trinity* or *completeness*. (see *Israel* and *Eliah*)

Eladah God has adorned, God is ornament, whom God clothes

Elah oak; terebinth; [while oak (in a desert environment) evokes images of rest or shade; terebinth is a small tree which yields turpentine, though both symbolize the product of 'earth'].

Elam youth; remote time; hidden; eternal; [in Akkadian = highland]

Elasah, Eleasah God is doer, whom God made, God has made

Elath, Eloth [c] palm grove; a grove

El-beth-el [c] God of the house of God, the house of God; [it symbolizes a state of consciousness in which our Higher Self controls all our thoughts]

Eldaah whom God called, God desires

Eldad God is a friend; whom God loves

Elead God is a witness, whom God praises, God has witnessed

Elealeh [c] God is exalted, whither God ascends, God has ascended

Eleasah (same as *Elasah*)

Eleazar God is helper, whom God aids, God has helped

El-Elohe-israel [c] God, the God of Israel [An affirmation meaning that only *El* can be the God of those who are on the path towards God Realization (i.e. Zion)]

Eleph [c] union, ox

Elhanan God is gracious; whom God gave

Eli Jah is high; height; [possibly an abbreviation of *Eli'el*, meaning: God is exalted, or of *'Eliah*: Jah is exalted]. (It is a name of a high priest).

Eli (or **Eloi**) my God; [in Matthew 27:46 using a quotation from Psalm 22:1].

Eliab God is father, whose father is God, my God is a father

Eliada, Eliadah God is knowing, whom God cares for, God knows

Eliah El is Jah. [This stipulates that the *Existing One*
(*Jehovah*) and *El* (the Divine Presence and the
unifying principle within our consciousness) are One.
Later (in John 10:30) Jesus avers the same principle by
saying: "I and my Father are one". Jesus, of course, is
speaking from the *El*, or *Christ Consciousness* 'point
of view']. (see *Elijah*)

Eliahba God hides, whom God hides, God will hide

Eliakim God is setting up, (whom) God establishes

Eliam God is founder of the people, my God is a kinsman
(same as *Ammiel*) (see *people*)

Elias (Gr. form of *Elijah*)

Eliasaph God is gatherer, (whom) God (has) added

Eliashib God is requiter, (whom) God restores

Eliathah God has (or is) come, to whom God comes, my
God comes

Elidad God is a friend, whom God loves, my God loves

Eliel God is God; El is my God; to whom God is strength;
[A most powerful symbol. Compare: I AM THAT I
AM. *Eliel* reinforces the name (or the invocation)
Eliah stating that from human point of view, the only
God we can attain to is *El*, the Divine Presence *within*
us, that which we call the Higher Self] (see *Eliah,
Elijah*)

Elienai unto God are mine eyes, unto Jah my eyes are
raised, my eyes are towards Jah

Eliezer God is help, my God is help

Elihoenai (see *Elioenai*)

Elihoreph God of harvest rain; to whom God is the reward;
[God of autumn?]

Elihu God himself, whose God is He, my God is He

Elijah God is Jah, God himself, my God is Jah; [Again a
most powerful symbol of the Divine Principle which
we must find and maintain within our consciousness.
It stipulates again that *El* is in fact one with Jehovah,
the *Existing One*]. (see *Eliah, Eliel*)

Elika God is rejector; [whom God purifies?]

Elim [c] palm trees, oaks, large trees; [the 2nd encampment of Israel after they crossed the Red Sea. Whichever tree we choose, all symbolize the products of 'earth', i.e. Israel is still firmly entrenched in physical consciousness].

Elimelech God is (my) king; to whom God is king

Elioenai to Jah are mine eyes; unto Jah my eyes are turned

Eliphal God is judge, whom God judges, God has judged

Eliphalet God is escape, to whom God is salvation or deliverance

Eliphaz God is dispenser; to whom God is strength; [possibly: God is fine gold] (see *gold*)

Elipheleh(u) Jah is distinction, whom God distinguishes, God distinguishes him

Elisabeth (from the Hebrew: *'Elîsheba*) God is swearer, to whom God is the oath, my God is fulness

Elisha God is saviour; to whom God is salvation

Elishah God saves

Elishama God is hearer, whom God hears, (my) God has heard.

Elishaphat God is judge, whom God judges, my God has judged

Elisheba (Hebrew name for *Elizabeth*)

Elishua God is rich; God is salvation (same as *Elisha*)

Eliud my God is majesty, God is my praise; God of the Jews; (from the Hebrew: *Elîhôd*)

Elizaphan God is protector, (whom or my) God protects or conceals, God of the hidden

Elizur (my) God is a rock

Elkanah God is possessing, whom God possessed, God has redeemed or created

Elkoshite my bow is God, bow of God

Ellasar [c] strong rebelion, oak of Assyria. [City of Arioch: *lion like*? The temples discovered were to the God of the sun, and the Sumerian name is *Arawa* that means: abode of light.]

Elmodam (same as *Almodad*)

Elnaam God is delight and fulness, God is gracious, God is pleasant, whose pleasure is God

Elnathan God is giving, to whom God gave, God has given

[*Elohim*] variously translated as: God, god, goddess, gods, judges, great, mighty, very great, angels, objects of worship. Whichever translation, it is evocative of *the Power within*, the *El* of the human equation in Its many manifestations. (see *El*)

Eloi (or **Eli**) my God; (see *Eli*)

Elon oak, strong, strong man; terebinth

Elon-beth-hanan [c] oak (or terebinth) of the house of grace

Elonites belonging to Elon (see above)

Eloth (**Elath**) oak or terebinth grove or a large tree

Elpaal God is working, to whom God is the reward, God has wrought

Elpalet, Eliphalet God is escape, to whom God is salvation or deliverance

El-paran oak (or mighty tree) of Paran; [Paran = *full of caverns*]

Eltekeh [c] God is Teke; whose fear is God, fear of God

Eltekon [c] God is firm; whose foundation is God

Eltolad [c] God is begetter, whose prosperity is from God, God shall cause to bear

Elul the gleaning month; [the 6th month of Jewish religious year, beginning with the new moon of August or September].

Eluzai God is strong, God is my praises, God is my strength

Elymas a sorcerer; a wise man; [a false prophet] (see *Bar-Jesus*)

Elzabad God is endowing, whom God gave, God has given

Elzaphan God is protecting, (whom or my) God protects or

119

conceals

emerald or turquoise, a green-colored, transparent variety of beryl. It symbolizes Divine Life

Emims the terrible; terrible (or frightening) men; [a race of giants]. They symbolize "giants" or idols, creations of man's mind, which we treat as real and become terrified of them.

Emmanuel (see *Immanuel*)

Emmaus [c] mineral springs

Emmor (see *Hamor*)

Enam [c] double (two) fountains

Enan fountains; having eyes

En-dor [c] spring of habitation, fountain of dwelling; fountain of Dor; (Dor = *circle, dwelling*)

Eneas [from Hebrew: praise of Jah]

En-eglaim [c] fountain of two calves

enemies symbolize our negative thoughts, e.g.: fears, doubts, belief in limitation. (see *wicked, heathen*.)

En-gannim [c] fountain (or spring) of gardens

En-gedi [c] fountain (or spring) of the kid (i.e.: young goat)

En-haddah [c] swift fountain; fountain of sharpness (i.e. swift fountain)

En-hakkore [c] swift fountain (or spring) of the crier or of him that calls; [or spring of the partridge]

En-hazor [c] fountain of the village

En-mishpat [c] fountain of judgement

Enoch, Henoch tuition, teacher, dedicated one, initiated, [experienced?]

Enos, Enosh a mortal; a man

En-rimmon [c] fountain (or spring) of the pomegranate

En-rogel foot fountain, fountain of the fuller; [spring of the spy?]

En-shemesh fountain (or spring) of the sun

En-tappuah fountain (or spring) of the apple-tree

Epænetus, Epenetus laud-able, praiseworthy

Epaphras lovely

Epaphroditus filled with love
Ephah obscurity, darkness; [also a dry measure]
Ephai obscuring; languishing, tired
Epher young deer or calf or gazelle
Ephes-dammim [c] extension of brooks; boundary of
    blood
Ephesus [c] desirable; [Diana, goddess of the moon (*the
    subconscious*) had been worshipped by the Ephesians.
    Note: Greek word *ephesos* means: desirable].
Ephlal judging; judgement
Ephod 1. oracular 2. priestly garment, (attached to the
    ephod was a breastplate...)
ephphatha be opened
Ephraim [also c] doubly fruitful; [also the name of the
    north gate to Jerusalem]
Ephrain [c] hamlet; [same as Ephron]
Ephratah, Ephrath [c] fertility, fruitfulness; (the ancient
    name for Bethlehem-Judah)
Ephron strong; of or belonging to a calf; [young gazelle?]
Epicureans [Followers of Epicurus: a Greek philosopher
    who defined his philosophy as the art of making life
    happy with intellectual pursuits as well as physical
    pleasure, in moderation. He relied on experience as
    test, not on reason, and denied the existence of gods].
Er watcher, watchful
Eran vigilant, more watchful
Erastus beloved, desirable
Erech [c] length, size; (The city with its surrounding area
    was a necropolis of the Assyrian kings).
Eri my watcher, watchful, my watchful one
Esaias (Greek form of *Isaiah*)
Esar-haddon victorious, conqueror; (the god) Assur has
    given a brother
Esau hirsute, hairy; red. [Esau symbolizes Jacob's lower or
    animal nature, i.e. the material consciousness]
    (compare *Adam*)

Esek contention; strife
Eshbaal a man of Baal; [later called *Ish-bosheth* = man of shame]
Eshban man of understanding; man of wisdom; son of fire.
Eshcol [also c] a cluster (of grapes etc.)
Eshean [c] a slope; support
Eshek strife; oppression
Eshtaol [c] hollow way, searching out
Eshtemoa [c] obedience; place where the oracle is heard; listening post
Eshtemoh [c] (same as preceding)
Eshton rest; womanly
Esli separated from God; (probably same as *Azaliah*)
Esrom (same as *Hezron*)
Esther star, the planet Venus; happiness; [The Persian name for *Hadassah* that means: myrtle]
Etam [c] wild beasts' laird, a place of ravenous creatures; a bird of prey
Etham [c] boundary of the sea; desolation, extremes of habitation; [The 2nd station after Israel left Egypt said to be on the edge of the wilderness].
Ethan firm, enduring, firmness; ancient; permanently (flowing with water)
Ethanim the perennial, [from a Phoenician word referring to the streams which had still borne water in this, the 7th (i.e.: dry) month of the Hebrew religious year which began with the new moon of September or October. The first month of the Jewish religious year was in spring].
Ethbaal with Baal or Baal's man; living with Baal
Ether [c] riches, fullness, plenty; perfume
Ethopia (region of) burnt faces; (Greek word for the Hebrew *Cush*)
Ethnan a gift, give or hire
Ethni my gift; bountiful; [probably shortened from *Ethnan*]
Eubulus good counselor, well advised

eunuch [an officer] It symbolizes a mindset which lost capacity to increase life in all its forms (a consciousness which lost it's awareness of the Creative Spirit)

Euodias success; fragrance; prosperous journey

Euphrates bursting, sweet; [the fertile river?] (see *Pison*)

Euroclydon [united winds of Eurus and Aquilo] a strong northeast wind

Eutychus fortunate

Eve life, life-giving; [Eve, being a woman, symbolizes (an inexperienced) soul, i.e. psyche. Thus it is the soul which gives life to the body (Adam), although ultimately it is (the redeemed) 'Adam' who becomes the Christ]. (see *Adam*)

Evening symbolizes fear, belief in limitation, (imaginary) problems.

Evi desire

evil is never a 'thing' or 'entity' in its own right. It symbolizes the *absence* of, or the inability to realize, the Presence of God; it also describes the loss of belief in the Christ (the I AM) within. [No less than 12 different words in Hebrew and Greek are all translated to mean 'evil'].

Evil-merodacha man of Mero-dach, man of (the god) Marduk (a Babylonian god).

exodus departure

eye is the organ with which we detect (or gather) light, i.e. Knowledge. It symbolizes the ability to focus our attention. Thus a **single eye** symbolizes the need to keep our attention on the acquisition of Divine Knowledge. [One could make a reference to the "spiritual eye", which the mystics place adjacent to the pineal gland, but the symbolic meaning would remain the same].

Ezar help, helper; treasure

Ezbai shining, beautiful, blooming

Ezbon splendor

Ezekias (Greek form of *Hezekiah*)

Ezekiel God is strong, (whom) God will strengthen

Ezel division, separation, departure

Ezem [c] strength, mighty; bone

Ezer help

Ezion-gaber backbone of the mighty one; backbone of a
     giant; [the last station of Israel before entering the
     'holy wilderness' of Zin].

Ezion-geber (same as preceding)

Eznite strong, sharp; one belonging to Etsen

Ezra help, assistance, [or abbreviation of *Azariah* = Jah has
     helped]

Ezrahite belonging to Ezrach, a native

Ezri my help; the help of Jah

F

face symbolizes the power of recognition (e.g.: of God's
     omnipresence)

false witnesses symbolize thoughts resulting from negative
     conditioning embedded in one's subconscious.

fasting In the Gospel of Thomas, Jesus, employing the
     colloquial meaning of the word, states: "if you fast you
     will beget sin to yourselves." Thus, when advocated,
     fasting refers to abstinence from negative thoughts,
     particularly thoughts of limitations, not to abstaining
     from comestibles. [For discussion of fasting see
     Kapuscinski Stanislaw, *Key to Immortality*, logion 14.]

father often symbolizes "the worshiper", e.g.: Abiner,
     meaning *father of light* would symbolize "one who
     worships (divine) knowledge"

Father (in heaven) The Spirit, the Higher Self, the Divine
     Presence. (see *El*)

feeble knees symbolize fear
Felix happy
female symbolizes our (man's and woman's) emotional
   nature. It also symbolizes our subconscious mind.
   (see *woman, male*)
Felix happy
Festus joyful
fire (and brimstone) 'fire' generally and particularly 'fire
   and brimstone', symbolize the power of the cleansing
   action of Spirit.
firmament the Hebrew word *raqia* means expanse or
   expansion. [For discussion of the above see
   Kapuscinski Stanislaw *Beyond Religion I, Genesis,*
   [Inhousepress 1998, '01, '02; Smashwords 2010]
fish is a symbol of wisdom; it served as an early Christian
   symbol of recognition. It is also a sign of the Zodiac
   (Pisces), occupying the segment between the signs of
   Ram (Aries) and the Gardner (Aquarius). [Later the
   pope, bishops and abbots wore a headdress in the
   shape of a fish's head as a sign of office].
flesh symbolizes the manifestation, the sum total of that
   which one is, i.e.: the physical body with all its
   allegiances; in a higher (more developed)
   consciousness it symbolizes the Spiritual(ized) Body,
   i.e.: the conscious individualization of Spirit upon the
   waters, i.e.: upon the human soul. Particularly a flood
   of (imaginary) misfortunes. N.B.: In the spiritual or
   Biblical sense, all misfortunes are imaginary. Spiritual
   reality (the state of consciousness towards which we
   are all climbing) is always perfect.
floods symbolize stormy (mental) experience
foes symbolize negative thoughts; (see *enemies*)
fortress Depending on context a *fortress* symbolizes: 1. a
   consciousness which is closed to spiritual ideas (a
   walled city). or 2.a state of consciousness which is
   both safe and powerful, (see *ark*)

fortification (see preceding)

Fortunatus prosperous, fortunate

forty is used as an *indefinite* number, e.g. an uncertain period of time, but long enough to accomplish the necessary task; (compare: *forty days, forty years*)

forehead symbolizes the intellect; [the mental awareness]

fourth man (the) in a some allegories, the *fourth* man symbolizes the spiritual nature, i.e. the true Self

G

Gaal scarab; rejection, loathing; [scarab was a black winged dung beetle, or an image of one, held sacred by the Egyptians]

Gaash quaking, shaking; [symbolizes traumatic experiences]

Gaba [c] height; hill

Gabbai ingatherer; a collector of tribute

Gabatha elevated place; height

Gabriel God is mighty; man of God; [a divine messenger, Angel, sent to Daniel, Mary and Zacharias]. Gabriel symbolizes the state of consciousness susceptible to inspiration, i.e. the influence of the Spirit.

Gad the seer, lot, fortune, good fortune; a troop

Gadarenes people of Gadara, fortunate, organized

Gaddi, Gadi belonging to fortune, fortunate, my fortune

Gaddiel Gad is fortune bringer, fortune sent from God, God is my fortune

Gadite (the) patronymic of the tribe of Gad.

Gaham blackness; burning brightly; [sunburnt?]

Gahar prostration, concealment, hiding place; born in (the year of) little rain

Gaius the early one; gladness, rejoicing

Galal great, rolling; [worthy?]

Galatia land of the Gauls (the ancient people of France); white as milk

Galeed heap of witness; witness-heap

Galilee [c] the circle, circuit, region, cylinder; (see *circle*)

Gallim [c] heaps or fountains

Gallio one who lives on milk; white as milk (see *Galatia*)

Gamaliel God is recompenser, benefit of God, God has rewarded

Gammadim variously translated as "pigmies, warriors, giants" as well as "guards or watchmen"

Gamul weaned, matured, rewarded

Gareb reviler, despiser; scabby

Garmite the strong or bony one

Gashmu corporealness; (born in) the rainy season; (same as *Geshem*)

Gatam burnt valley or field

gates symbolize new understanding; (see *doors*)

Gath [c] wine press, fortune

Gath-hepher [c] the wine press of the well

Gath-rimmon [c] the wine press of the pomegranate

Gaza [c] the strong place; fortress, (a Philistine city, same as *Azzah*)

Gazer precipice, place cut off; cutter

Gazez shearer

Gazithites, Gazites inhabitants of Gaza or Azzah

Gazzam devourer, swaggerer; eating up

Geba [c] height, hill

Gebal [c] border; hilly, mountain

Geber strong; man

Gebim [c] springs, cisterns, ditches; trenches

Gedaliah Jah is great; whom Jah has made great

Gedeon (Greek form of *Gideon*)

Geder [c] walled; wall

Gederah [c] sheepcote, inclosure, sheepfold; a walled place; (see *sheep*)

Gederoth [c] sheepcotes, sheepfolds, enclosures

G

G

Gederothaim [c] two sheepfolds, two enclosures
Gedor [c] wall or pockmarked
Gehazi denier, diminisher; valley of vision
Geliloth [c] circles; regions
Gemalli camel owner
Gemariah Jah has completed, Jah has accomplished (it)
generation symbolizes accumulated thought patterns, i.e. a
    mind-set. (see *people, men,* etc.)
Genesis the birth, begetting; (first book of the Bible){For
    discussion of the creative process see Kapuscinski
    Stanislaw *Beyond Religion I*, *Genesis*, [Inhousepress
    1998, '01, '02; Smashwords 2010]}
Gennesareth (lake) [In the Old Testament it is called the
    sea of Chinnereth or Cinneroth. Elsewhere it is
    referred to as the sea of Galilee and the lake (or sea) of
    Tiberias. (see *sea*)
Gennesareth (land) garden of the prince; valley of riches.
Gentiles nation, a collective body; (Hebrew *goi*; Greek
    ethnos); symbolizes everyone, regardless of religion,
    who is not an Israelite, i.e. not (as yet) on the spiritual
    path.
Genubath theft; stolen goods; [weaned?]
Gera enmity; a grain
Gerah a bean, or grain, or kernel, or a small coin
Gerar [c] circle; sojourning
Gergesenes organized, assembled
Gerizim [c] 1. waste places; 2. persons living in a desert
Gershom, Gershon a stranger there; expulsion, sojourner
    or banishment, [from the word *garash* meaning: to
    drive out]
Gesham or **Gershan** firm, strong; unclean
Geshem corporealness; (born in) the rainy season; [Greek
    word *gesam* = rain, storm].
Geshur [c] bridge-land; bridge
Gether [dregs?]

Gethsemane [c] wine press and oil (farm); oil press
Geuel God of salvation; majesty of God
Gezer [c] precipice; cutter
Gezirete dwelling in the desert land
Giah [c] gushing forth, bubbling spring, waterfall, ravine
    or glen
Gibbar high, mighty, manly or a hero
Gibbethon [c] height; a lofty place
Gibea highlander; hill
Gibeah, Gibeath [c] height; hill
Gibeon [c] hill, height; pertaining to a hill
Giddalti I have magnified (God); I have increased
Giddel very great, gigantic, He (God) has made great
Gideon feller, hewer, i.e. great warrior; one who cuts down
Gideoni cutting down, my hewer; warlike
Gidom [c] a cutting off or desolation, cut off
Gihon stream, gusher, a river; (see *Pison*)
Gilalai rolling, weighty; [dungy?]
Gilboa bubbling fountain, hill country; [Note that the
    apparent contradiction in the literal sense is strangely
    compatible when interpreted from the symbolic point
    of view...]
Gilead [c] strong, hard, rocky, rough; hill of witness
Gilgal [c] circle, wheel, the (stone) circle; (see *circle*)
Giloh [c] circle; exile; uncovered
Gimzo [c] sycamore; a place abounding with sycamores
Ginath protection; garden
Ginnetho, Ginnethon great protection; garden
Girgashite (c) (those) dwelling in a clayey soil; condensed
Gispa, Gishpa listening, attentive; flattery
Gittah hepher [c] wine-press of the well
Gittaim [c] two wine presses
Gittite inhabitants of Gath
gittith from or of Gath; [a musical instrument
    manufactured in Gath].
Gizonite cut stone, [a pass?]

Goath, Goah [c] constance; lowing, crying out

Gob pit, pool, hollow, cistern, ditch

God (s) This word is used in the Bible as a translation of Hebrew *El, elah, elohim, eloah, Jehovah* (read by Jews *elohim*, probably Yahweh), Greek *theos, kurios* (Lord, master), *theodidaktos* (God taught), and a number of other terms. Only the context can help the student to determine the intent of the original writer.

God of Jacob symbolizes the Power that enables us to redeem our soul.

God of Shadrach... illustrates the power of I AM (*El*) over most dire circumstances.

Gog high, mountain; stretched out, extended

Golan [c] circle, circuit, exile, [dust and sand?]

gold symbolizes the omnipresence of the all-powerful God. [Not to be confused with *golden images* and idols which are mistaken for the symbol of the Truth that lies behind them].

Good Shepherd symbolizes the Christ within, the I AM. It is He who looks well after the sheep: i. e.: thoughts.

Golgotha a scull; [Not a mountain but an 18-foot high hill] (see Calvary)

Goliath an exile or soothsayer; [a giant: taking a *cubit* at 21 inches, he would rise to 10.5 feet in height! His battle with David symbolizes the power of Divine Love over a phenomenon of physical consciousness, regardless of the latter's apparent 'magnitude'].

Gomer completion, perfection, complete; heat

Gomorrah [c] fissure, submersion; oppression

Goshen [c] drawing near; [Only MBD offers a translation] {A fertile land where the Hebrews dwelt while in Egypt. It could be the same as the land of Ramses (*the land of the sun*), or a district of it}.

Gospels generally accepted as the highest expression of Christ's message. The format itself also serves to illustrate the fourfold nature of man. Matthew's symbolizes the physical, Luke's the emotional, Mark's the intellectual and John's the spiritual nature of man. [Somewhat misleadingly, Matthew is represented by a man or an angel, Luke by an ox, Mark by the lion and John by the eagle. It has been suggested that the various gospels had not been written by men bearing their names. Such a contention may be of vital interest to historians, but has no bearing for the seekers of *spiritual* truth]

government symbolizes princely power over thoughts and the state of consciousness; [in some cases it refers to the usual meaning of the word, i.e. a steering, directing or simply lordship or power].

Gozan food; protion

grass (as that which grows out of the earth) symbolizes (the product of) conscious aware-ness; [in a poetic sense, *grass* to people living in the desert must surely symbolize riches or blessings beyond compare] (see *trees*)

Grecia Greece

green pastures symbolize an abundance of spiritual ideas within a peaceful state of consciousness. (see *grass*)

Gudgodah [c] cave of Gidgad, incision; [thunder?] [A station of the Israelites in the wilderness also called *Hor-harridgad*].

Guni protected; painted with colors; spotted sand grouse

Gunites family of Guni

Gur [c] dwelling, sojourn; a lion's whelp

Gur-baal [c] dwelling of Baal; [possibly *tur Ba'al* = the rock of Baal]

H

Haahashtari the courier; the muleteer (mule driver)
Habaiah Jah is protection, whom Jah hides, Jah has hidden
Habakkuk love's embrace or embracer
Habaziniah Jah is exuberant; glory of Jah, [lamp of Jah?]
Habor united, joining together
Hachaliah Jah is hidden; whom Jah disturbs
Hachilah draught; dark
Hachmoni the wise, a wise one
Hachmonite "son of Hachmoni" (see above)
Hadad 1. mighty, (the name of an ancient Semitic god of storm); 2. sharp, pointed
Hadadezer mighty is the help; whose help is (the god) Hadad
Hadadrimmon Hadad of Rimmon (i.e. of pomegranate)
Hadar enclosing, fire god, powerful; inclosure; (same as *Hadad?*)
Hadarezer Hader is help; (same as *Hadadezer*)
Hadashah [c] new (city)
Hadassah myrtle, joy; gladness
Hadattah [c] new; [an appellation of *hazor*: enclosure]
Hadid [c] peak, sharp
Hadlai lax, rest, a stout one
Hadoram Hadar is high, majestic
Hadrach [c] periodical return; [possibly a Syrian god of the seasons]
Hagab bent; locust
Hagaba, Hagabah (same as preceding)
Hagar wandering, flight, emigration; fugitiave
Haggai, Haggi festive, one born on a feast day, my feast
Haggeri wanderer, fugitive
Haggiah festival or feast of Jah
Haggith festive, festal
Hai [c] the heap; [same as *Ai*]

Hakkatan the little one; the small

Hakkoz the nimble; the thorn, briar

Hakupha incitement

Halah [c] moist surface(?)

Halak the smooth or bare (mountain)

Halhul [c] full of hollows; anguish

Hali [c] necklace, ornament

Hallohesh, Halohesh the whisperer; the enchanter ;
   ornament

hallelujah (see Alleluia)

Ham swarthy, dark coloured; warm; [Note: 1. The
   Egyptian *Kem = Ham*, as an adjective means black *and*
   warm. 2. Noah's son, by this name, symbolizes the
   intellect].

Haman magnificient; splendid; famed; only; noise;
   arrogance; trouble; the celebrated Haman, Hom; (see
   Hammedatha)

Hamath, Hemath [c] defenced, walled; fortress

Hamath-zobah fortress of Zobah

Hammath [c] warm (or hot) springs

Hammedatha who troubles the law; given by Hom; [if of
   a Persian origin: 'given by the moon']

Hammelech the king, councelor

Hammoleketh the queen

Hammon [c] hot springs; warm

Hammoth-dor [c] warm (or hot) springs of Dor.
   [Appointed a city of refuge. Compare the cities of
   Hammath and *Hammon*]

Hamonah multitude, noise

Hamon-gog multitude of Gog

Hamor large jackass

Hamuel (Hammuel) God is a sun; heat (wrath) of God

Hamul pity, pitied, who has experienced mercy

Hamutal God is fresh life, kin to the dew, refreshing like
   dew, my father is the dew

Hanameel God is kind, gift or grace of God, whom God

graciously gave

Hanan merciful, grace, gracious

Hananeel God is gracious; whom God graciously gave; [another form of *Hanameel* above]

Hanani gracious; [probably same as *Hananiah*]

Hananiah Jah is gracious, whom Jah graciously gave

hand symbolizes the power of manifestation or the ability to express spiritual ideas on the physical plane.

Hanes [c] (possibly) Mercury; banishment of grace.

Haniel God is gracious, favor of God, God is kind to me

Hannah grace, gracious, graciousness

Hannathon [c] dedicated to grace, gracious, favored

Hanniel (same as *Haniel*)

Hanoch, Henoch dedicated founded; straitened; arrested; instructed.

Hanun whom (God) pities, pitied; gracious

Haphraim [c] double (two) wells or pits

Happizzez (same as *Aphses*)

Hara [c] hill country, mountainous

Haradah [c] terror, fear; [the 20th station of the Israelites in the wilderness, 9th from Sinai]

Haran strong, enlightened; sanctuary, mountaineer. [Note: in the spiritual sense, he who climbs a mountain, i.e. raises his consciousness, becomes strong and enlightened and finds sanctuary from his problems].

Hararite a mountaineer; (see preceding)

Harbona, Harbonah ass-driver

Hareph early born; plucking; harvested

Hareth thicket; engraved

Harhaiah Jah is protecting; [dried up?] [Other sources give Hebrew *Charchaiah* = hot anger of Jah; *Charhaiah* = Jah diminishes]

Harhas glitter, splendor

Harhur nobility, distinction; inflammation; (born during) a fever (of the mother)

Harim snub-nosed, flat-nosed; dedicated

H

Hariph early born; autumnal showers; harvest

Harnepher snoring; panting; snorting; breathing hard (through the nose). [Possible transliteration of *Hob Charnepher*, the Egyptian *Hr nfr* = (the god) Horus is good].

Harod terror, trembling, spring of terror

Haroeh the seer

Harosheth [c] forest; carving; ["Harosheth of the Gentiles" so named from the mixed races that inhabited it].

Harsha magician, artificer, enchanter, the silent (or the deaf) one

Harum elevated; [high?]

Harumaph flat-nosed, having a split nose

Haruz industrious, active, gold or diligent

Harvest symbolizes the result of one's endeavors, be they in the physical, mental or spiritual consciousness.

Hasadiah Jah is kind, whom Jah loves, Jah is (or has been) gracious

Hasenuah the violated, she that is hated, the hated one; [The name is *Senuah* prefixed by the definite article]

Hashabiah Jah is associated, whom Jah esteems, Jah has taken account (i.e.: of childlessness and bestowed a son)

Hashabnah Jah is friend, Jah has thought of me

Hashabniah (same as *Hashabnah*)

Hashbadana understanding to judge

Hashbad(d)anah (same as preceding)

Hashem shining; fat; wealthy

Hashmonah fruitfulness, fatness, fat soil; [The Israelites' 25th station in the wilderness, 24th from Sinai]

Hashub, Hasshub associate, thoughtful, thought of or regarded (by God), considerate

Hashubah association, consideration, esteemed; (same as preceding)

Hashum shining; rich

Hashupha (see *Hasupha*)

Hasrah splendor; glitter; (another form of *Harhas*)
Hassenaah the thorn hedge, the thorny; [Senaah = hated?]
(see *Hasenuah*)
Hasupha nakedness; [Arabic: *hashuf* =swift]
Hatach a gift; the inner part; verity. [Same as *Hathach*, a
Persian name]
Hathath bruised; terror; weakened.
Hatipha seized, carried off as captive, taken
Hatita exploration, digging, smooth, pock or pustule
marked
Hattil decaying; wavering; [Arabic *hatila* = to be
talkative]
Hattush contender; assembled, gathered together
Hauran cave district, hollow land, [broad depression or
black-land?]
Havilah stretch of sand, circle, district
Havoth-jair [c] tent villages of Jair; (see *Jair*)
Hazael God sees, whom God watches over, God has seen
Hazaiah Jah is seeing, whom Jah watches over, Jah has
seen
Hazar–addar [c] Addar-town; [town of the fire-God?],
strong enclosure, noble (or wide) village {*hazar* is
variously translated as: town, village, enclosure and
court. It invariably symbolizes a specific state of
consciousness, which derives from the context in
which it is used.}
Hazar–enan [c] court (or enclosure) of the fountains,
fountain-town, or village etc.
Hazar–gaddah [c] court of Gad, luck-town, enclosure or
village of good fortune
Hazar–hatticon [c] middle Hazar, middle-town (or
village)
Hazar–maveth [c] court (or village) of death, death-town
Hazar–shual [c] fox or jackal village, jackal-town (see
Idalah?)
Hazar–susah [c] horse-village, mare-town

Hazar–susim [c] horses-town, enclosure for a mare; (same as preceding)

Hazazon sandy surface; (see *Hazeson*)

Hazelelponi protection of the face of; the shadow looking on me, overshadow my countenance

Hazerim [c] villages, courts

Hazeroth [c] enclosures, settlements

Hazezon–tamar [c] row of palms; pruning of the palm; [*hazazon* = sandy surface + of *tamar* = the palm tree]

Haziel God is seeing, the vision of God, God sees

Hazo vision, seer, (God) sees him

Hazor [c] enclozure, enclosed, castle

Hazor hadattah [c] new court or village

head particularly a human head symbolizes the Christ Truth, (or at least our understanding of It) as distinct from blind faith and/or emotional groping; (see *forehead*)

heart symbolizes that which is firmly imbedded in our subconscious; (the purpose of prayer is to reprogram the subconscious by a process that takes place in the conscious aspect of our awareness)

heathen (the) symbolize the negative thoughts; thoughts of limitation.

heaven symbolizes a spiritual state of consciousness, occasionally a state of bliss and contentment. It is also a spiritual 'storehouse' in which the redeemed qualities (virtues) are safeguarded, presumably until the next great circle of the Zodiac at which time they will be enhanced still further, in accordance with our heightened understanding. According to the Bible, there is no end of this process of edification, even as there is no end to infinity.

Heber 1. (1 Chronicles 5:13): shoot, production; 2. (Genesis 46:17): companion, associate, fellowship

Hebrew belonging to Eber, [a patronymic of Abraham]; (also given as one from the other side, a crosser, a nomad; [Further it is the language spoken by Jews in Palestine, the land of Canaan]. A Hebrew is a member of a race, and is not to be confused with Israel, which (in the Bible) defines and symbolizes a state of consciousness, which in turn is not to be confused with the present political entity.

Hebron [c] ford, company, alliance, association, place of covenant

heel symbolizes vulnerability (in our mind, emotions or physical body).

Hegai, Hege eunuch; separated; thought; meditation; [Eunuch placed in charge of young women might symbolize an "emasculated" male principle in charge of "young" i.e.: inexperienced souls]

Helah ornament, necklace, tenderness; rust

Helam [c] stronghold

Helbah [c] fertility, fatness

Helbon [c] fruitful, fertile

Heldai enduring; terrestrial

Heleb fat, fatness

Heled (same as *Heleb*); world

Helek portion (in the sense of a gift bestowed by God)

Helem strength

Heleph [c] place of rushes; exchange, change

Helez strength; liberation, (God) has delivered

Heli (Greek form of *Eli*)

hell [c] symbolizes a state of consciousness devoid of (any) awareness of the Presence of God.

Helkai Jah is a (or my) portion; portion of Jah

Helkath a portion (of land), field, plot of ground

Helkath-hazzurim [c] field of rocks, or flints, or sword edges

Helon strong, valorous, power

Hemam ranging, destruction, confusion

Heman faithful

Hemath 1. (1 Chronicles 2:55) fortress; 2. (Amos 6:14)

warmth

Hemdan pleasant, desirable

Hen grace, kindness, favor

Hena [c] low land

Henadad Hadad is gracious, favor of (the god) Hadad

Henoch (see *Enoch* and *Hanoch*)

Hepher a well, a pit, a digging

Hephzibah my delight is in her, in whom is my delight

Heres [c] heat, the sun

Heresh work, silence, silent, dumb, skillful, artificer

Hermas, Hermes Mercury, interpreter (of the gods)

Hermogenes born of Mercury

Hermon [c] prominent, rugged, lofty, banned or sacred (mountain)

Herod offspring of a hero, like a hero; (King of Judaea 37 B.C. - 4 A.D., married 10 times, ordered massacre of all small children, executed 3 of his own sons...).

Hesed kindness, mercy, (God has kept) faithfulness

Heshbon [c] device, reckoning, account, counting; stronghold

Heshmon [c] fruitfulness; fatness

Heth terrible, terified; [*Hettites*: sons of Heth?]

Hethlon [c] lurking place, stronghold, hiding-place, wrapped -up

Hezeki my strength (i.e.: God), [possibly a contraction of *Hezekiah*]

Hezekiah Jah is strength, the might of Jah, Jah has strengthened

Hezion vision

Hezir returning home; swine, wild pig, boar

Hezrai blooming, beautiful; inclosed wall, having a fixed habitation (from Arabic: *hadari*?).

Hezro, Hezron blooming; [same as preceding]

Hiddai the rejoicing of Jah, splendor (of Jah), mighty chief

Hiddekel rapid; [The Hebrew name for the (Greek word) *Tigris*, from Persian: *Tigra*]. (see *Pison*)

Hiel God is living, God lives, [God is a brother?]

Hierapolis priestly city a sacred or holy city

Higgaion thought, reflection, meditation, solemn sound

high place (invariably) a place where the Hebrews offered sacrifices, i.e.: prayers. It symbolizes a state of raised consciousness, i.e.: the practice of the Presence of God (which is the essence of the teaching of the Bible)

Hilen [c] strong place, sandy; (same as *Holon*)

Hilkiah Jah is protection, portion of Jah, Jah is my portion

hill symbolizes the uplifted consciousness. It is thus a symbol of spiritual power achieved through prayer. (see *mountain, high place, hill,* etc.)

hill of the Lord the realization of Christ within. A state of awareness of the Higher Self. Also referred to as 'His holy place'.

Hillel praised greatly, praising, he has praised

Hinnom [valley of the sons of Hinnom] In the New Testament it is referred to as Hell (*gehenna*), a state of consciousness devoid of any awareness of the Presence of God.

Hirah distinction, nobility, good, excellent

Hiram devoted (to God), (my) brother is exalted, noble

Hivite (s) villager, midlander; (physical existence?) [In Hebrew the word is always used in the singular, thus it could refer to a progenitor or a locality. Hebrew: *hawwah* = tent-village; Arabic: *hiwa* = collection of tents].

Hizkiah, Hizkijah Jah is strong, might of Jah, Jah has strengthened

Hobab beloved

Hobah [c] lurking place, a hiding-place, reed country, on the left hand i.e.: north (when facing east; (see *east*)

Hobaiah (see *Habaiah*)

Hod glory, splendor, majesty (of God)

Hodaiah honorer of Jah, praise of Jah

Hodaviah Jah is his praise, praise (or thank thee) Jah

H

Hodesh (born the day of the) new moon; (see *moon*)
Hodevah Jah is honour, praise Jah; (see *Hodaviah*)
Hodiah, Hodijah (same as preceding)
Hoglah magpie; partridge
Hoham Jah protects the multitude; (see *multitude*)
holiness symbolizes wholeness (physical, emotional,
    mental and spiritual completeness)
Holon [c] strong place; sandy; (see *Hilen*)
Homam raging, destruction; (see *Hemam*)
Hophni strong, pugilist; [also consider Hebrew word
    chophnî from Egyptian *hfn/r* that means: tadpole]
Hophra priest of the sun, the heart of Ra rejoices
Hor mountain, a height
Horam elevated, height
Horeb waste; desert; [This translation seems inconsistent
    with the symbolism expressed elsewhere in the Bible.
    In Exod. 3:1, Horeb is referred to as the *mountain of
    God*, thus signifying state of highly raised
    consciousness, rather than a "desert"]
Horem [c] fortress, sacred, enclosed
Hor-hag(g)idgad [c] hill of the cleft, hollow (or cavern or
    cave) of Gidgad; [The Israelites' desert station].
Hori free, noble; cave dweller
Horim, Horites troglodytes; descendants of Hori
Hormah [c] fortress; a devoting, a place laid waste,
    devoted, accursed
horns symbolize power, or the signs of power. Ten horns:
    the executive or enormous power.
Horonaim [c] double caves; two caverns
Hosah [c] refuge, refugee, [fleeing to Jah for refuge?]
horses In the book of Revelation black, red and dun horses
    symbolize the intellectual, emotional and physical
    aspects of human nature. The white horse symbolizes
    our spiritual aspect. The concept of man's fourfold
    nature goes back (at least) to the Egyptian god Horus
    and his 4 sons. It reappears in the story of Noah and

his 3 sons and later in the story of Shadrach, Meshach, Abednego and the fourth man. There are ample examples of it in the Revelation of John. It continues in the Christian tradition in the Christ's halo being divided into four (the redeemed aspects).

Hosea Jah is help, Jah helps, salvation

Hoshaiah whom Jah set free, Jah saves, Jah has saved

Hoshama Jah is hearer, Jah has heard

Hoshea (Oshea) Jah is help, Jah saves

hosts (the) symbolize the abundance of thoughts [good or bad] invading our mind; (see *nations*)

Hotham, (Hothan) determination; signet ring, seal

Hothir abundance

house symbolizes a state of consciousness (see *city, Beth*)

House of the Lord symbolizes a *raised* state of consciousness, the profound awareness of unity with our Higher Self. (see *hill of the Lord*)

Hukkok [c] ditch; decreed, hewn in, carve**Hukok** [c] ditch; (see *Helkath*)

Hul circle, circling

Huldah weasel, mole

Humtah [c] enclosed place, [fortress?] reptile, place of lizards

Hupham protected; inhabitant of the shore

Huppah protection, sanctuary

Huppim protection, (Jah is) covering; secret

Hur free, noble; whiteness, cavern; [also offered as a derivative of the Egyptian god Horus, and/or of the Akkadian word *huru* that means: child]

Hurai linen worker, a weaver of linen; purifier; the rejoicing of Jah; [possibly same as *Hiddai*]

Huram free noble; [same as Hiram]

Huri linen weaver or worker

Hushah haste

Hushai quick, hasty, [the brother is a gift?]

Husham hasting, haste

Hushim hasting, those who make haste; fleeting
Huz firm
Huzzab established, it is decreed; [also variously offered
  as: 1. the name of a Hotham queen, 2. a poetic form
  for Ninevah, and 3. to mean "mistress"]
Hymenæus nuptial; belonging to Hymen (the god of
  marriage)

I

I AM symbolizes the Divine Presence, the Individualized
  Soul, the Christ Consciousness, the High or Higher
  Self.
Ibhar whom God chooses, he (God) chooses, chooser
Ibleam [c] place of victory, He destroys the people;
  people's canal
Ibneiah Jah is builder, whom Jah will build up, Jah builds
  up (i.e.: grants prosperity) **Ibnijah** (same as preceding)
Ibri passer over, Hebrew; {In *logion 42* of the *Gospel of
  Thomas* Jesus says: *Become passers-by*. For discussion
  on the implications of this statement refer to KEY TO
  IMMORTALITY by Stanislaw Kapuscinski}.
Ibzan splendid; shining; (active?)
Ichabod where (is) the honour (or glory?) inglorious, glory
  is departed
Iconium [c] image-like; likeness, likely; yielding; retiring
  giving away; breast of sheep; {Gleamed from MBD}
Idalah [c] memorial to God; [snares?], jackal; [Note that
  the Egyptian god *Anubis* was symbolically portrayed
  as a jackal]
Idbash stout, corpulent; honeyed, honey, honey-sweet
Iddo 1. festal, opportune; 2. favourite; 3. honourable.
  [Also given as: *loving* and *seasonable* in different
  contexts. It is to be noted that the Hebrew writing is

I Dictionary of Biblical Symbolism / Stanislaw Kapuscinski

different though the translators give the same English spelling of the word].

idol(s) symbolize false creations of our mind. It is not a statue or a painting we worship, but the *image* it represents to us. The Bible condemns *all* forms of idolatory. (see below)

idolatry (see *adultery*)

Idumea (Greek form of *Edom*)

Igal, Igeal deliverer; whom God will avenge, he redeems, may (God) redeem

Igdaliah Jah is great; whom Jah shall make great

Iim [c] circles, heaps; ruins. [The 37th encampment of the Israelites in the wilderness since leaving Egypt, 26th from Sinai]

Ije-abarim [c] heaps of the further region; ruinous heaps of Abarim; (one of the later encampments of the Israelites in the wilderness)

Ijon [c] heap; a ruin

Ikkesh subtitle; perverseness of mouth, crooked

Ilai elevated; most high

Illyricum [c] joy, rejoicing

image (graven) see *idols*

Imla, Imlah fulfilling, whom (God) will fill up, he (God) fills

Immanuel God (is) with us. [Symbolic name given to the child who was announced to Ahaz and the people of Judah as the sign that God would deliver them from their enemies. According to Isa. 7:14 & Matt. 1:23, it is also the prophetic name of Jesus Christ] (see *child,* see *Judah,* see *enemies*)

Immer projecting, prominent; talkative; lamb, sheep

Imna he withholds, whom (God) keeps back, he (God) defends

Imnah prosperity, he counts, good fortune, [whom (God) assigns?]

Imrah He (God) contends, (is) stubborn, he resists; height of Jah

Imri projecting thought, eloquent, Jah speaks; (from *Amariah*)

incense burning of incense symbolizes the process of transmutation from lower to higher nature.

India land of Hindu or Sindhu; occult; praise; whisper. [The limit of the territories of Ahasuerus in the east, and Ethiopia in the west]

Iphedeiah Jah is freeing, whom Jah frees, Jah redeems

Ir watcher; city

Ira watcher; watchful

Irad self-leading passion; blind whirling; fugitive; wild ass; dragon. {Gleamed from MBD}

Iram belonging to a city

Iri Jah is watcher; belonging to a city

Irijah Jah is seeing, whom Jah looks on, Jah sees (or provides)

Ir-nahash [c?] serpent city, magic city, snake-town

Iron [c] place of terror; reverence

Irpeel God (is) healer, restored by God, (which) God heals

Ir-shemesh [c] city of the sun

Iru watch; belonging to a city

Isaac laughter, he laughs; [Isaac symbolizes the soul (psyche) in the process of unfolding, thus a receptive state of mind]. **Isaiah** Jah (is) helper, salvation of Jah, Jah saves, Jah has saved

Iscah Jah (is) looking

Iscariot man of Kerioth; man of city; [or from the root *shakar* (to deceive) = the false one, the deceiver]

Ishbah appeaser, he praises, soothes, praising, may (God) be calm and allay (his wrath)

Ishbak free, overcome

Ishbi-benob dweller on the mount, one who dwells at Nob (nob = *high place*)

Ish-bosheth man of shame

Ishi 1. (Chronicles) my help; salutary. 2. (Hosea) my

husband

Ishiah, Ishijah Jah exists; whom Jah lends, may Jah forget (my sin or misfortune)

Ishma high, elevated; [contraction of *Ishmael*?]

Ishmael God (is) hearing, whom God hears, God hears, may God hear

Ishmaiah Jah (is) hearing, (whom) Jah hears

Ishmerai Jah (is) keeper, whom Jah keeps, Jah watches

Ishod man of honour, man of glory

Ishpan firm, strong; [cunning?] [Perhaps from *Ishpah* meaning: may God judge?]

Ish Tob [c] man (men) of Tob; [Tob = *fruitful, good*].

Ishuah, Isuah self-answering; level, equal of birth (or worth)

Ishui, Ishuai, (as preceding?) [also *Isui* and *Jesui*]

Island when used symbolically, it is that which is *land* within the *water*. (see *land*, see *water*)

Ismachiah Jah (is) supporter, whom Jah upholds, Jah supports

Ismaiah Jah (is) hearing, Jah hears

Ispah firm, strong; bald

Israel ruling with God, soldier of God, God contends. *Is* symbolizes the feminine principle [soul or psyche], *Ra* [Egyptian sun god] represents the masculine principle, *El* symbolizes the Divine Principle – the wholeness of Trinity. Thus Israel symbolizes a soul fully aware of its divine nature and actively seeking God, (regardless of religion of cultural affiliation.

Israelite symbolizes anyone who is actively seeking God

Issachar bearing hire, reward, there is hire

Isshiah (see *Ishiah*)

Isuah, Isui (see *Ishuah, Ishui*)

Italy [c] island of the fish (or of lamb?)

Ithai being, existing; plowman; [or shortened from *'ittîahu* (Ittiah) meaning: with me is Jah, or from *ittîel* (Ithiel) meaning: with me is God]

Ithamar island of palms
Ithiel God is, God is with me
Ithmah purity; bereavedness; orphan
Ithnan [c] strong place, con-stant, perennial
Ithra excellence, (God is or gives) abundance
Ithran excellent, (super) abundance; [same as *Ithra*]
Ithream remnant (remainder) of the people, the (divine) kinsman has been liberal (or abundant).
Ithrite belonging to Jether (Jether = *pre-eminent*)
Ittah-kazin kindred of the extremity; time of the chief, [or Hebrew *Eth-qasîn* meaning: time of the ruler]
Ittai being, living; oneness; plowman; (see *Ithai*)
Iturea [probably derived from *Jetur*, the son of *Ishmael*]
Ivah [c] hamlet; or the god of Iva, (sky?)
Izhar, Izehar he (God) shines, shining; oil
Izrahiah Jah (is) appearing, whom Jah brought to light, Jah shines
Izri creator, former; descendant of Jezer, [Jah has formed?]

J

Jaakan, Jakan intelligent; one who turns
Jaakobah to Jacob, he (God) protects, deception
Jaala, Jaalah elevation; wild she-goat, mountain goat, ibex
Jaalam whom God hides, youth, young man
Jaanai whom Jah answers, may God hear, answerer
Jaare-oregim foresters; forest-ers of the weavers
Jaasau maker, he makes
Jaasiel, Jasiel God is maker, whom God created, God (El) makes; (See *El*)
Jaazaniah Jah is hearing, whom Jah hears, Jah hears
Jaazer, Jazer [c] whom (God) aids, he helps; fortified
Jaaziah Jah is determining, (whom) Jah strengthens
Jaaziel God is determining, (whom) God strengthens

Jabal moving; [possibly: sprout, leader of stream]

Jabbok running, flowing, pouring out; [Arabic: *bakka* = to give abundantly, to split]

Jabesh [c] dry place; dry

Jabesh-gilead [c] Jabesh of Gilead

Jabez [c] height; causing pain; [name connected with "sorrow" and/or "pain"].

Jabin intelligent; whom he (God) considered, he understands, perceives

Jabneel [c] God is builder, may God cause to be built, God causes to be built

Jabneh [c] building; whom (God) causes to be built

Jachan afflicting; troubled

Jachin whom (God) strengthens, he (God) establishes, founding

Jachin (the pillar) The right hand pillar at the entrance into the temple of Solomon symbolizes the mathematical unity of the cosmos. (see *Boaz*) {Gleaned from Emmet Fox *DIAGRAMS FOR LIVING*, © 1968 by Harper & Row. (pg.38)}

Jacob following after, supplanter. [Jacob symbolizes a soul aware of its spiritual nature, but not yet aware of its divine origin. As Jacob's consciousness expands, he becomes (is renamed) Israel].

Jada knowing, wise, he knows (or cares)

Jadau favourite, friend

Jaddua very knowing, skilled, known

Jadon judging, a judge, he judges, Jah rules

Jael chamois; [or same as *Jaala*: mountain goat, ibex]

Jagur [c] dwelling; a lodging

Jah [Yah] a poetic form of Jehovah [YHWH = Yahweh or Yehovah]: *the Existing One*: I AM THAT I AM. (see *Jehovah*)

Jahath comfort, revival

Jahaz, Jahaza [c] a place trodden down, open space

Jahaziah Jah reveals, whom Jah watches over, Jah sees

Jahaziel God reveals, whom God watches over, God sees

Jahdai whom Jah directs, Jah leads; leader, guide

Jahdiel union of God, whom God makes glad, God gives joy

Jahdo union, he has been made happy (by God), may God rejoice

Jahleel God awaits, hoping in God, may God be friendly

Jahmai Jah protects

Jahzah trodden down; [same as *Jahaz*]

Jahzeel, Jahziel God apportions or distributes, whom God allots

Jahzerah Jah protects; may he bring back

Jair Jah enlightens; Jah arouses

Jair forest

Jairus he enlightens; (Greek form of *Jair*)

Jakan (see *Jaakan*)

Jakeh pious, cautious, hearkening

Jakim a setter up; (God) sets up, raises up or establishes

Jalon Jah abides; passing the light

Jambres to be refractory, rebellious

James (English equivalent of Jacob)

Jamin the rightside (i.e.: south), right hand, prosperity, fortune

Jamlech Jah rules, he makes to reign, he grants dominion

Janna oppression; affliction; (possibly another form of John)

Jannes rebelion; deception; (one who with *Jambres* withstood Moses)

Janoah [c] resting place, rest, he rests, quiet

Janohah [c] (same as preceding)

Janum [c] propagation; sleep, toslumber, to be drowsy

Japheth the extender, extension, let him make wide; or fair, or beauty; [this Noah's son symbolizes the emotional nature of man].

Japhia high, splendid, he shines, may (God) cause to shine

forth
Japhlet Jah causes to escape, may he deliver, he will
    deliver
Japho [c] high; beauty
Jarah honeycomb; unveiler; forest
Jareb contender, avenger; one who is contentious
Jared, Jered descending, descent; servant, slave
Jaresiah Jah gives a couch; whom Jah nourishes; Jah
    plants
Jarha increasing moon; filing moon; adoption; {Gleamed
    from MBD}
Jarib striving, adversary, he strives, may (God) contend or
    plead
Jarmuth [c] height
Jaroah new moon; [to be soft, thin?]
Jashen shining; sleeping; (see *Hashem*)
Jasher upright, the righteous one
Jashobeam (may) the people return,
Jashub turning back, he returns, may (God) return
Jashubi-lehem turning back to Bethlehem, bread shall
    return; [giving bread?]
Jasiel (see *Jaasiel*)
Jason healing; helping; [Greco-Judean equivalent of
    Joshua]
Jathniel God is giving, God gives, God is constant
Jattir [c] wide; excelling, pre-eminence, abundance
Javan Greece; Ionia; the East; warmth; fertility; soil; mire;
    deception; [wine?] [The oldest name for Greece]
Jazer (same as *Jaazer*)
Jaziz shining; he strengthens; [wanderer?]
Jearim woods, forests
Jeaterai steadfast
Jeberechiah Jah is blessing, whom Jah blesses
Jebus, Jebusi [c] trodden down
Jecamiah Jah is standing, Jah establishes, Jah will establish

Jecholiah Jah is able, Jah is strong, Jah has prevailed

Jeconiah, Jechnias Jah (is) establishing, Jah establishes

Jedaiah 1. Jah is praise, Jah praises; 2. Jah (is) knowing, Jah knows

Jediael God knows; known of God

Jedidah beloved

Jedidiah Jah is friend; beloved of Jah

Jeduthun a choir of praise, praise; [friendship?]

Jeezer (contracted from *Abiezer*)

Jegar-sahadutha the heap of witness (or of testimony); a heap of stones as testimony; [The name given by Laban to the heap of stones that Jacob called Galeed, which is the Aramaic and the Hebrew terms for *the heap of witness*].

Jehaleleel God is praised, he praises God, God praises

Jehdeiah union with Jah, whom Jah makes glad, Jah is glad

Jehezekel God is strong, God strengthens, God will strengthen

Jehiah Jah (is) living, Jah lives

Jehiel God is living, God lives

Jehizkiah Jah is strong, the might of Jah, Jah strengthens; (same as *Hezekiah*)

Jehoadah Jah unveils, whom Jah adorns, Jah has decorated

Jehoaddan Jah gives delight, Jah makes glad, [Jah is beauteous?]

Jehoahaz Jah upholds, whom Jah holds fast, Jah has grasped (my hand), Jah has laid hold of

Jehoash Jah supports, Jah has given; (same as *Joash*)

Jehoaz (contracted from *Jehoahaz*)

Jehohanan Jah is (or has been) gracious

Jehoiachin Jah establishes, Jah has established

Jehoiada Jah knows

Jehoiakim Jah sets up, Jah has set up, Jah raises up, Jah will establish

Jehoiarib Jah pleads (or contends), Jah will contend, may

151

Jah plead (or contend).

Jehonadab Jah is liberal (bounteous or noble); (see *Jonadab*)

Jehonathan Jah gives, Jah has given; [same as *Jonathan*]

Jehoram Jah is high, Jah is exalted

Jehoshabeath Jah makes oath, Jah is the oath (i.e.: the faithful One); (see *Jehosheba*)

Jehoshaphat Jah is judge, (whom) Jah judges, Jah has judged

Jehosheba (see *Jehoshabeath*)

Jehoshua, (Joshua) Jah saves, Jah is salvation (or deliverance)

Jehovah The Existing One, the Eternal One, Self-Existent; [The incommunicable name of the God of Israel. In the Common Version of the English Bible it is generally *improperly* translated by "the Lord"]. Jehovah is an anglicized version of the personalized God of the Old Testament, coming from the Hebrew letters: *Yod, Hé, Wau, Hé*, (the tetragrammaton YHWH), which four letters represent the masculine and feminine principles. It is also written as *Yahweh* and is abbreviated as Jah] {Charles Fillmore, who is credited with having compiled the MBD, recommends than whenever we read *Lord* in the Bible, we should substitute *I AM*. [MBD page 332]}

Jehovah-jireh [c] Jah will see (or provide), Jah sees (or provides)

Jehovah-nissi Jah is my banner

Jahovah-shalom Jah is peace, Jah sends peace

Jehozabad Jah gives (or endows), Jah gave (or has bestowed).

Jehozadak Jah is just

Jehu Jah is he (i.e.: God)

Jahubbah hidden, he (God) hides

Jehucal, Jucal Jah is able, Jah is mighty (or powerful)

Jehud [c] honorable; praise; (shortened from *Judah*)

Jehudi a Jew; of Judah; my celebration; my praise; my honor; my thanksgiving.

Jehudijah a Jewess, the Jewish one

Jehush he (God) comes to aid, may he aid, to whom God hastens; collector, helper

Jeiel God snatches away, God has remembered; God unifies; [God has kept?]

Jekabzeel [c] God gathers

Jekameam standing of the people, may (the) kinsman establish, the (divine) kinsman will raise up.

Jekamiah Jah is standing, Jah establishes, Jah will rise up (or estalbish); may Jah establish.

Jekuthiel God is mighty, the fear of God, may God nourish sustain (or sustain).

Jemima pure, fortunate, day; dove

Jemuel God is light, day of God

Jephthae, Jephthah God opens, he opens, God will open (or set free), Jah will open

Jephunneh he turns, may (God) again be turned (favorably), for whom it is prepared; appearing

Jerah the moon

Jerahmeel God is merciful, whom God loves, may God have compassion

Jered low, flowing, descent, servant

Jeremai Jah is high, dwelling in heights; [abbreviation of Jeremiah]

Jeremaiah Jah is high, Jah is exalted (or exults, or loosens), whom Jah has appointed (or established)

Jeremias (Greek form of *Jeremaiah*)

Jeremoth elevation, high places, swollen, thick

Jeremy (shortened English form of *Jeremiah*)

Jeriah, Jerijah Jah is foundation, whom Jah regards (or sees)

Jeribai Jah contends (or pleads); contentious

Jericho [c] fragrant; a fragrant place; moon-city, city of the moon (god); [the latter translations pertain to the subconscious. In its context, the "moon-city" symbolizes intellectual understanding].

Jeriel foundation of God, founded by God, God sees

Jerijah (same as *Jeriah*)

Jerimoth elevation, high places, [Hebrew: *jerîmôt* = swollen]

Jerioth tremulousness; tent curtains

Jeroboam enlarger; may the people multiply, may (God) increase the nation, whose people are many; (see *people, nation*)

Jeroham loved, who is loved, may he have compassion or be pitied (by God)

Jerubbaal contender with Baal, let Baal plead (or contend)

Jerubbesheth contender with the idol; let shame plead, (another designation for the preceding: -*besheth* = shame, instead of -*ba'al* = lord) [Another name of Gideon, given to him by those who wished to avoid pronouncing the name of Baal. A good example of the Biblical teaching that words are thoughts, and thoughts are things which affect the state of consciousness).

Jeruel foundation of God, founded by God. [It is interesting that a desert or a wilderness is recognized as a symbol for the foundation of God (-*el*), or perhaps, a starting point in one's evolution. In other words, the state the consciousness is in when *El* starts Its work. We cannot start with preconceived ideas.]

Jerusalem [c] possession of peace, founded on peace, foundation of (God) Shalem (i.e.: peace). [Jerusalem symbolizes the highest state of consciousness short of God realization (see *Zion*) wherein peace prevails. It is the highest a human consciousness can rise by its 'own' efforts.

Jerusha, Jerushah possession, possessed

Jesaiah, Jeshaiah Jah is helper, Jah saves, Jah has saved, deliverance of Jah; (same as *Isaiah*)

Jeshanah [c] ancient; old (city?); listless, inactive
Jesharelah Jah is righteous
Jeshebeab seat of the father, father's seat, may the father
    enjoy a long life; [Note: this does not refer to the
    'heavenly' father]
Jesher rightness, uprightness
Jeshimon [c] a waste, a desert, barren desert
Jeshishai Jah is ancient, like an old man, old, decrepit;
Jeshohaiah humbled by Jah, whom Jah humbles
Jeshua, Jeshuah Jah is help, Jah is salvation
Jeshurun, Jesurun the darling upright, righteous, the
    upright one; [A poetical appellation of the people of
    Israel]
Jesiah Jah exists; (see *Ishiah*)
Jesimiel God sets (up), God establishes (or places); [whom
    God founds?]
Jesse Jah exists; he who is; upstanding; firm; upright; [a
    man of Jah? gift?]
Jesui Jah is satisfied; (same as *Ishua*)
Jesus saviour; deliverance through Jah; [from the Hebrew:
    Yeshûa (Jeshua), the late form of *Yehôshûa*, meaning:
    Jah is salvation].
Jether pre-eminent; God is (or gives), abundance; (same
    as *Ithra*)
Jetheth subjection
Jethlah height, lofty
Jethro pre-eminence, excellence; [also called *Reuel* =
    friend of God] (same as *Ithra*)
Jetur an inclosure
Jeuel God (El) has remembered; snatching away; [God has
    saved?]
Jeush collector; [same as *Jehush*]
Jeuz counsellor, helper; he (God) comes to aid, may he aid,
    may he protect
Jew [Hebrew: *Hehûdî*] a descendant of Juda; in later times
    also (erroneously) an Israelite. It should be well

understood that in the biblical sense the Israelites,
Jews and/or Hebrews are *not* synonymous.

Jewry Judea, (the land of Judah: *praised*)

Jezaniah Jah determines, Jah harkens (or hears), [Jah
adorns?]

Jezebel without cohabitation; unmarried; where is prince?
(Jezebel symbolizes a self-centered soul given to
sensuality and material concerns).

Jezer formation, anything made, form or purpose

Jeziah Jah unites, whom Jah assembles, may Jah purify

Jeziel God unites, assembly of God; [may God sprinkle,
i.e. purify? God gathers?]

Jezliah Jah delivers; long living, [deliverance?]

Jezoar splendid; he is yellowish-red

Jezrahiah Jah is shining, Jah shines forth, Jah will shine
(or arise)

Jezreel [c] God sows, God scatters

Jibsam lovely sweet, fragrant, perfume

Jidlaph melting away; he is sleepless, [weeping?]

Jimnah, Jimna prosperity; (same as *Imnah*)

Jiphtah [c] breaking through; God (he) opens, (same as
Jephthae)

Jiphthah-el God is breaking through, which God opens

Joab Jah is father

Joah Jah is brother

Joahaz Jah helps, whom Jah holds, Jah has grasped, Jah
strengthens, Jah has laid hold of

Joash Jah has bestowed, Jah supports, whom Jah supports,
Jah has given

Joatham (Greek form of *Jotham*: *Jah is perfect, Jah is
upright*)

Job 1. (Genesis 46:13): returning; a desert. 2. (Job 1:1)
hated; one persecuted, where is (my) father

Jobab howling, lament, a desert

Jochebed Jah is honour (or glory)

Joed Jah is witness, for whom Jah is witness

Joel Jah is God

Joelah God is snatching; let (God) avail; [He helps?]

Joezer Jah is help

Jogbehah [c] height, lofty, elevation

Jogli exiled, an exile, may God reveal

Joha Jah is living, Jah lives

Johanan Jah is (or has been) gracious

John Jah is gracious; [English way of spelling *Johanan*. Possibly a form of Jona or Jonah, probably from Yôchanan or Yehôchanan meaning: Jah is gracious]. (Also, see *Jonah*)

Joiada Jah knows

Joiakim Jah sets up, Jah establishes (or raises up); [shortened from *Jehoiakim*]

Joiarib Jah contends (or pleads)

Jokdeam [c] anger of the people; burning of the people

Jokim Jah sets up (or establishes); (shortened from *Jehoiakim*)

Jokmeam [c] standing of the people

Jokneam [c] possessed by the people, possession of the people

Jokshan fowler, ensnarer

Joktan little, small one, younger son (or brother)

Joktheel [c] God's reward of victory, subdued by God, [God is perfection?]

Jonadab Jah is bounteous or generous or liberal; [same as *Jehonadab*]

Jonah a dove; [a symbol of a promise of peace]

Jonas, Jona (Greek form of the Hebrew *Jonah*)

Jonath-elem-rechokim "A silent dove far off" or "A dove of the far off oaks" (A title of Psalm. 56).

Jonathan Jah has given, whom Jah gave; (same as *Jehonathan*)

Joppa [c] height, beauty

Jorah harvest-born; [watering? early rain?] (see *Hariph*)

Jorai Jah teaches; whom Jah teaches; instructed of Jah;

rain from Jah.

Joram Jah is high; (same as *Jehoram*)

Jordan descender, flowing down; (The great river of
Palestine, rising from two springs in the valley
between Lebanon and Hermon)

Jorim Jah is exalted, Jah is hight; (a form of *Joram?*)

Jorkeam spreading the people; [spreading of the people?]

Josabad, Jozabad (see *Jehozabad*)

Josaphat (Greek form of *Jehoshaphat*)

Josedech Jah is righteous, Jah is just; (same as *Jehozadak*)

Joseph increaser, he shall add, may he (God) add

Joses (a Greek form of Joseph) One of the brothers of
Jesus. [Those intent on destroying the *symbolic* beauty
of the *Virgin Mother* (which defines the state of the
soul, not a physiological condition), should bear in
mind that Mary may well have given birth a number of
children, (James, Joses, Simon and Judas as well as a
some daughters, see Matt. 14:55 & 56)].

Joshah Jah is gift, Jah's gift

Joshaphat Jah judges, Jah has judged [shortened from
Jehoshaphat] **Joshaviah** Jah dwells (within him), Jah
is equality

Joshbekashah seated in hardness, seat of hardship

Joshua, Jehoshua Jah saves, Jah is salvation (or
deliverance); [Symbolizes the unfolding realization of
the I AM, the Indwelling Christ. In a person-alized
form the name Joshua means *leader* or *saviour*]

Josiah (whom) Jah heals; Jah supports

Josias (Greek form of *Josiah*)

Josibiah Jah causes to dwell, to whom God gives a
dwelling, may Jah dwell

Josiphiah Jah adds, whom Jah will increase, may Jah add
(other offspring)

Jotbah [c] excellent for water; pleasantness or goodness

Jotbathah, Jotbath [c] (meaning as above) [the 29th
encampment of Israel from Egypt, the 18th from Sinai]

JothambJah is perfect, Jah is upright
Jozabad Jah gives (or endows), Jah gave (or has bestowed)
Jozachar Jah remembers, (whom) Jah has remembered
Jozadak Jah is great, Jah is just; (same as *Jehozadak*)
Jubal playing; nomad; stream; [music?]
Jucal able; Jah is mighty, (same as *Jehucal*)
Juda, Judah, praise, praised, let him (God) be praised
Judas (Greek form of *Judah*)
Jude (an abbreviation of *Judas*) **Judea** (see *Jewry*)
Judges (in the Book of Judges), from the Hebrew *shofetim*
    meaning: champions, rescuers or leaders (often in
    guerrilla warfare).
Judith Jewess; [the feminine form of Judah, i.e.: let him
    (God) be praised
Julia soft-haired; downy; (fem. form of *Julius*)
Julius soft-haired; downy; curly.
Jupiter father Jove (i.e.: Zeus-pater); A chief Greek and
    Roman deity.
Jushab-hesed kindness is returned; whose love is returned
Justus upright, just or righteous
Juttah [c] extended, inclined; (also see *Jotbah*)

K

Kabzeel [c] God gathers, God has gathered; (same as
    Jekabzeel)
Kadesh [c] holy, consecrated, a holy place
Kadesh-barnea [c] (as preceding)
Kadmiel God the primeval, God is the ancient One;
    [eternity of God?]
Kadmonites eastern, oriental, children (or people) of the
    east (see *people, east*)
Kallai Jah is light; swift
Kanah [c] a reed, or possession; a place of reeds (a

designation of a brook *and* a city)

Kareah, Careah bald

Karkaa [c] floor, deep ground, bottom

Karkor [c] soft even ground, deep ground; [plain?]

Karnaim [c] two horns

Kartah [c] city

Kartan [c] double city, town or city

Kattath little, insignificant

Kedar powerful; black (or dark, or swarthy) -skinned

Kedemah eastern, eastward, towards the east

Kedemoth [c] eastern parts (or regions)

Kedesh [c] holy, sanctuary, sacred place

Kehelathah [c] (place of) assembly; called together; convocation; [18th station of Israel from Egypt, 7th from Sinai] {Israel's stations are confirmed by the *Analytical Concordance to the Bible* by Robert Young, LL.D.}

Keilah [c] inclosed; [sling?]

Kelaiah Jah is light; [contempt?]

Kelita poverty, littleness; dwarf

Kemuel God stands (or rises), congregation of God, God has raised himself, [God's mound?]

Kenan (see *Cainan*)

Kenath [c] possession

Kenaz, Kenez side, flank; hunting

Kenite belonging to Ken (Kain or Cain)

Keren-happuch horn for (or of) paint, horn of antimony (i.e.: a cosmetic case)

Kerioth, Kirioth [c] cities, hamlets, villages

Keros bent, stooped; [crook?]

Keturah fragrance, incense, perfumed

Kezia cassia; [the symbolic meaning suggested is: *acceptance*]

Keziz border; cut off; [*Emek-keziz* = the cut off valley, or a vale of fissure].

Kibroth-hattaavah [c] graves of lust (or of craving); [the 12th encampment of Israel in the desert, and the 1st from Sinai]

Kibzaim [c] double gathering, two heaps; grasping with both hands

Kidron turbit, dirty, dark

Kinah [c] smithy; song of mourning, lamentation, dirge

king The Hebrew *melek* (meaning counsellor, prince *and* king) is almost invariably translated as *king*, though perhaps *counsellor* might often offer a more interesting spiritual meaning – particularly since the title of a king might suggest one who has control over his psyche, particularly his subconscious.

King of glory Symbolizes the realization of God consciousness.

kingdom Symbolizes any established state of consciousness – thus kingdom can refer to a negative as well as positive state of consciousness, depending on the content of thoughts ruling or being preponderant in such a "kingdom". That is why the *kingdom* can only be: "within you".

Kingdom of God Symbolizes a state of consciousness beyond limitations.

kinsman symbolize thoughts, particularly those related to the aspirations of one who is of Israel. (see *people*)

Kir [c] wall, town, city

Kir-hareseth [c] brick-town; (see *stone*)

Kir-haresh (-heres) [c] (as preceding)

Kirioth [c] (see *Kerioth*)

Kirjath city (of); [contracted from Kirjath-jearim]

Kirjathaim [c] double city, twin city; [could it symbolize a split personality? Or perhaps a consciousness which attempts to serve "two masters"]

Kirjath-arba [c] city of Arba (Arba = *strenght of Baal*), fourfold city; [the latter suggest a symbol for the fourfold nature of man] (see *horses*)

Kirjath-arim [c] (contracted from Kirjath-jearim)
Kirjath-baal [c] city of Baal
Kirjath-huzoth [c] city of the outplaces, city of streets
Kirjath-jearim [c] city of forests (or of woods)
Kirjath-sannah [c] city of instruction; city of thorns
Kirjath-sepher [c] city of books, book-city, city of writing
    or of scribe(s); (see *Debir*)
Kish bow, power; [gift?]
Kishi bow of Jah, my gift; [trapper?]
Kishion [c] hard; hardness
Kishon, Kison bending, curving, winding, binding,
tortuous; the given one
Kithlish [c] separation; forti-fied; [later spelt: Chitlish]
Kitron [c] shortened, little; burning, smoke; [enclosed?]
Kittim (see *Chittim*)
Koa prince; [people named as enemies of Jerusalem]
Kohath assembly
Kolaiah voice of Jah, Jah has spoken
Korah baldness, bald
Kore crier, reader; partridge
Koz the thorn; (see *Hakkoz*?)
Kushaiah bow of Jah; Jah has presented (or bestowed); [a
    longer form of *Kishi*]

L

Laadah set time, festival; [order?]
Laadan festive born; [put in or-der?]
Laban white, glorious
Lachish [c] height; impregnable
Lael God-ward, (devoted) to God, belonging to God
Lahad dark coloured; oppression; slow, sluggish
Lahai-roi of the Living one who beholds me; to the living
    is sight; (see *Beer-lahairoi*)

L

Lahmam [c] place of light; place of bread
Lahmi Bethlehemite; warrior; my bread
Laish [c] lion
Lakum [c] fortification, obstruc-tion
lama why
lamb lambs, like sheep, symbolize thoughts. Lambs, more so than sheep, symbolize spiritual ideas. [Perhaps is should be mentioned that in the spiritual sense, all 'spiritual' ideas are perfect, it is our perception of them that is inadequate. (see 1 Corinthians 13:12)].
Lamb of God as the Perfect Spiritual Idea, it symbolizes our Higher Self, with particular reference to the *redeemed* (human) consciousness. It defines a state oftotal control over the conscious *and* subconscious awareness, what is elsewhere called the Christ Consciousness or the perfect individualization of God. (see *above*)
Lamech overthrower, wild man; destroyer
land Symbolizes the "bare ground", the *tabula rasa* upon which we are to cultivate our spiritual consciousness. It is also where we demonstrate our capacity to realize the Presence of God.
Laodicea [c] judgment of people
Lapidoth lamps, lightnings; torches (i.e.: brightness)
Lasea [c] stony, hard
Lasha [c] bursting forth; fissure
Lasharon [c] the plain of Sharon; of the plain
Lazarus without help; whom God aids, God has helped; [Greek word from Hebrew: *'El'eazar*]
Leah weary, languid; cow or wild cow
Lebana, Lebanah whiteness; white
Lebanon (the) white, snowy; (a mountain so called as for most of the year it is covered with snow)
Lebaoth [c] place of lionesses; lionesses
Lebbeus, Lebbæus man of heart
Lebonah [c] frankincense, incense

Lecah addition, attached place; [journey?]
Lehabim flame coloured, red; flaming; [the ancestor of the Egyptian Lybians?]
Lehi jaw-bone
Lemuel Godward, God is bright, devoted to God, belonging to God; [another name of a king generally assumed to be Solomon].
Leshem [c] fortress; precious stone
Letushim oppressed, struck, the hammered, smith
Leummim people(s), nations
Levi joined or attached [associate?]
Levite descendant of Levi
Libertines freedmen; [The Jews freed by Rome to return to Jerusalem, where they had a synagogue].
Libnah [c] whiteness; [the 16th station of Israel from Egypt, 5th from Sinai]
Libni white, distinguished
Libya Put; [Greek name for the Hebrew: *Phut* meaning: *bow*]
Libyans bowmen; (same as *Lubim*)
light (the) symbolizes spiritual knowledge and understanding. Divine Light symbolizes the Source of all Knowledge.
Likhi Jah is doctrine; (God) has accepted me; [fond of learning?]
Linus flax
lion symbolizes a *known* (if considerable) difficulty to be overcome; (versus e.g. a *dragon* which lurks deep in our subconscious).
lion of God symbolizes one who has overcome such difficulties (see above), thus symbolizing a very high state of consciousness, equivalent to the city of peace, Jerusalem.
Lo-ammi not my people
Locust symbolizes the onslaught of negative thoughts that invade our mind and stifle any spiritual activity while

destroying the acquest of our (physical or conscious) awareness.

Lod [c] fissure; born; division; [strife?]

Lo-debar [c] no pasture; "a thing of nought"

Lord symbolizes the divine presence of God within, the indwelling Christ, in particular one's own knowledge of God. In the science of metaphysics the Lord is referred to as the Higher Self or the I AM (see *El*)

Lord of Hosts symbolizes the Higher Consciousness controlling our stream of thoughts. A synonym for Divine Power.

Lo-ruhamah not pitied, not having obtained mercy

Lot concealed, dark coloured, veil, envelop, wrap closely

Lotan a covering, veiling, covered

Lubims parched, thirsty; (also see *Libyans*. Also given as same as *Lehabim*)

Lucas, Luke light-giving; [A physician who travelled with Paul and is said to have written the third gospel and the Acts of the Apostles]

Lucifer shining (or brilliant) one; light-bearer. [A translation of *helel* applied by Isaiah to the king of Babylon, in reference to his glory and pomp, not to his spiritual stature].

Lucius of light; [a noble?]

Lud disire to bring forth; conception; striving; binging forth; creeation; birth; [strife?]

Luhith [c] table; abounding in boards; made of slabs (stone of planks); a place of tablets or planks.

Luke (see Lukas)

Luz [c] bending, curve; almond tree

Lycaonia place of wolves, a wolf

Lycia wolfish; wild

Lydda [c] strife; pregnancy

Lydia (name of a place and a woman) strife; contention; (childbirth?)

Lysanias ending sorrow (or sadness)

Lysias loosening; freeing
Lystra [c] (city of Lycaonia) liberating; that which frees

M

Maachah, Maacah depression; [royal? stupid? foolish?]
Maadai Jah is ornament; adorn
Maddiah Jah is ornament; ornament of Jah, Jah is a
    promise
Maai Jah is compassionate, Jah is a promise, Jah promises
Maaleh-acrabbim ascent of scorpions
Maarath [c] bare place, a treeless place, barren field
Maaseiah Jah is a refuge; work of Jah
Maasiai work of Jah; [same as *Amashai*?]
Maath smooth; polished; sharpened; scrap; small; few
Maaz counsellor; wrath; anger; [irascible?]
Maaziah strength of Jah, Jah is a refuge
Macedonia burning; elevation
Machbanai cloak (of Jah); thick; fat;
Machbenah knob, lump; [clad with a cloak?]
Machi wounded; [short for *Machir*?]
Machir salesman; sold
Machnadebai gift of the noble one
Machpelah winding, spiral form; a doubling, double cave
Madai middle
Madian (Greek form of *Midian*)
Madmannah [c] heap, dunghill
Madmen [c] heap, dungheap, dunghill
Madmenah [c] (as preceding)
Madon [c] district of the Dan; (place of) contention or
    strife
Magbish [c] fortress; congregating
Magdala (**Magadan**) [c] a tower, greatness;
 Magdalene (a woman of Magdala, called Mary)

M

Magdiel God is renowned, praise of God, God is excellence

Magog [Akkadian *mat gugu* = land of Gog; Sumarian *gug* = darkness; thus: "the land of darkness?" In the Revelation of Saint John the Divine (20:8), Gog and Magog are recognized as symbols of the enemies of God. Darkness always symbolizes the absence of divine light, i.e. of divine knowledge, i.e. of the Presence of God].

Magor-missabib terror is about, terror on every side, fear round about; (a symbolic name for *Pashur*)

Magpiash collector of a cluster of stars

Mahalah tenderness, mildness; disease, weak

Mahalaleel God is splendor, God shines forth, praise of God

Mahalath sickness, weakness; mild; [also: *a musical instrument / choir*]

Mahali sick, weak; [see *Mahli*]

Mahanaim [c] two camps

Mahaneh-dan [c] camp of Dan

Maharai Jah has hastened, swift, hasty, impetuous

Mahath seizing, dissolution; [taking hold?]

Mahazioth visions

Maher-shalal-has-baz "hasten the spoil, rush on the prey" or "the spoil hastens, the prey speeds". [A symbolic name given to a son of Isaiah]

Mahlah sickly, disease, weak; mildness; (same as *Mahalah*)

Mahli sick or weak; mild; (same as *Mahali*)

Mahlon mild; a sick person, sickness

Mahol dancer; dance

Makaz [c] end, a cutting off

Makheloth assemblies; meetings, [the 21st station of Israel from Egypt]

Makkedah [c] place of shepherds

Maktesh depression, a trough, a hollow, a mortar

Malachi messenger of Jah, my messenger (or angel)
Malcham their king; thinking; [also an idol of Ammonites]
   (see *Molech*)
Malchiah, Malchijah Jah is king, Jah's king, Jah is my
   king; (see *king*) **Malchiel** God is a (or my) king, God's
   king
Malchiram my king (i.e.: God) is exalted
Malchi-shua king of aid, my king is noble
Malchus counsellor, [Greek form of *Malluch*] (see *king*)
male symbolizes the intellect (the conscious) as against
   female (the subconscious) which represents the feeling
   nature. In the Genesis male and female symbolize the
   dual nature of everyone of us. (see *man, female*)
Maleleel (see *Mahalaleel*)
Mallothi Jah is speaking (or is splendid), I have proclaimed
Malluch counsellor, reigning; (see *king*)
Mammon wealth, riches, fullness, property; [symbolizes
   the acquisitions, and a mind-set controlled by, the
   physical consciousness]
Mamre [c] firmness, vigour; fatness
man symbolizes the conscious awareness, particularly as
   pertaining to all earthly or material matters. It is also
   symbolizes the male principle of *Ra*; (see *Israel*)
man child (a) symbolizes an embryonic consciousness
   which needs to be nurtured before it can blossom into
   full self awareness.
Manaen comforter
Manahath resting place, rest, settlement
Manahethites (**Menuhoth**) resting (as above)
Manasseh causing forgetful-ness, one who causes to
   forget, making to forget
Manasses (Greek form of *Manasseh*)
Maneh a weight; [$^1/_{60}$ of a talent = *maneh*]
Manoah rest, quiet
Maoch poor; [oppressed?]

M

Maon [c] habitation, dwelling

Mara bitter; sad; (see *Mary*)

Marah bitter; [1st station of Israelites east of the Red Sea].

Maralah [c] declivity; trembling

Maranatha "Our Lord has come", (or "will come", or "comes")

Mareshah [c] possession, capital; chief; shaking

Mark, Marcus brilliant; [Credited with having written the 2nd Gospel. Symbolizes the intellect].

Maroth [c] bitter fountains, bitterness; lordship

Marsena worthy, forgetful man

Martha lady, mistress

martyr [Greek word: *martus* or *martur* means **witness**].

Mary 1. (from Mara or Marah:) bitter; 2. (from Miriam, Greek form of Mary): fat, thick, strong; rebellion or insurrection (against limitation); 3. (from Egyptian *mryt*) the beloved one; 4. (from Maya): illusion;

Maschil understanding or intelligent, or rendering intelligent; (a Psalm title)

Mash (same as *Meshech?*)

Mashal [c] depressed; [a contraction of *Mishal* or *Misheal?*]

Masrekah [c] place of rivers; vineyard

Massa load or burden

Massah testing, trial, tempta-tion

Mathusala (Greek form of *Methuselah*)

Matred God is pursuer; pushing forward; [expulsion?]

Matri, (Matrites) Jah is watching; rainy

Mattan, Mattanah a gift; (see the following)

Mattaniah gift of Jah

Mattatha (Greek form of the above)

Mattathah gift of Jah

Mattathias (Greek form of the preceding)

Mattenai gift of Jah; liberal; (shortened from *Mattaniah*)

Matthan, Matthat gift; giving

Matthew gift of Jah; [English way of spelling *Mattithiah*, which is another form of *Mattathias, Mattithiah* etc.]

Mattithiah gift of Jah

Mazzaroth The twelve constellations (or signs) of the Zodiac. [Also identified with the planet Venus, the cluster of Taurus].

Meah a hundred

Mearah cave

Mebunnai built up, built (by God)

Mecherathite [one of David's valiant men] of the sword (the word of God?)

Medad love, beloved; (also compared to *Eldad*)

Medan judgement, contention, strong

Medeba [c] flowing water, water of leisure, gently flowing waters, full waters

Medes the middle, midst; [inhabitants of Media]

Media [c] middle land

Megiddo (Megiddon) [c] place of God; place of troops, place of great abundance

Mehetabel (Mehatabeel) God benefits (or gives benefit), God is doing good, God makes happy

Mehida famous

Mehir (God) has received; dexterity; price, accepted, hire

Meholathite the dancing or joyful

Mehujael struck (or smitten) by God, God is combating

Mehuman faithful

Mehunim (see *Meunim*)

Me-jarkon [c] waters of yellowness, green (or yellow) waters

Mekonah [c] foundation, a base, dwelling place

Melatiah Jah delivers, whom Jah freed (or has set free or delivered)

Melchi my king; [Greek form of *Melchiah*]

Melchiah (see *Malchiah*)

Melchisedek (Greek form of *Melchizedek*)

Melchi-shua (same as *Malchi-shua*)

Melchizedek my king is righteous; king of righteousness

Melea fullness; fully supplied; abundance; multitude

Melech king, counsellor; judge

Melicu counsellor; [same as *Malluch*]

Melita flowing with honey; sweetened with honey.

Melzar the overseer, steward; [Akkadian *massâru*: guardian or warden]

Memphis [c] place of Vulcan; temple of the good god (Osiris); [Also called Moph or Noph. A city in central Egypt thus probably symbolizing a material state of consciousness]

Memucan upright; true; honorable; authority; [perhaps from old Persian *magav* meaning: magian?]

men symbolize our thoughts; [they inhabit the "cites" i.e. our consciousness]. (see *people*)

Menahem comforter; compassionate

Menan (Menna) numbered

mene numbered; [explained by the text in Daniel 5:26: *Mene, Mene, Tekel U-Pharsin*: numbered, weighed and divided].

Meonenim [c] beclouded; covert; overcast; darkened; [perhaps from Old Persian: *magav* meaning: magian?] See also Nenycab abive]

Meonothai Jah's dwelling; my habitations

Mephaath [c] height, beauty, splendor

Mephibosheth utterance of Baal; destroying shame, he (of one) who scatters shame (see *Jerubbesheth*)

Merab increase; greatly multipied.

Meraiah revelation of Jah; contumacy, obstinate, rebellious

Meraioth revelations; rebellions, obstinate

Merari bitter, excited; [or from Egyptian *mrry* meaning: beloved?]

Merathaim double bitterness; double rebellion, rebellions; [The symbolic name for Babylon]

Mercurious (Mercury) Latin name for *Hermes*; [An Olympian god of many functions: such as commerce,

thieves and cheats, of luck (hence gamblers) of
eloquence as well as the conductor of souls to Hades]

Mered bold, rebellious, rebellion

Meremoth strong, firm; elevations

Meres worthy

Meribah [c] strife, contention; water of strife

Merib-baal contender against Baal, Baal (the lord)
contends

Merodach bold; [the Babylonian idol Marduk, the god of
war]

Merodach-baladan (see *Berodach-baladan*)

Merom [c] a high place, a height, elevation

Meronothite singer; crier

Meroz shrinking; becoming compact; firm; stable; secret
place; refuge; [calamity?]

Mesha freedom, deliverance, salvation

Meshach where is God? guest
of the king; withdrawn from the temple. [name given
to Michel, one of Daniel's companions. Sanskrit: mêshah =
a ram] (see Shadrach, horses)

Meshech, Mesech perceptibility; that which is not
peraceptible; drawing out; deducting; [tall ?]

Meshelemiah Jah recompenses (or repays), Jah has
recompensed

Meshezabeel God delivers; God is deliverer

Meshillemith recompense, restitutions, (divine) act of
recompense

Meshillemoth recompenses, retribution; (as preceding)

Meshobab returned, brought back, delivered, converted

Meshullam associate, friend, recompensed

Meshullemeth restitution; (feminine of preceding)

Mesobaite station of Jah; where Jah is standing

Mesopotamia amidst (or between) the rivers

Messiah anointed, an anointed one; [derived from *msh*
meaning: "touch lightly" or "rub with oil", i.e.: anoint]

Messias (Greek form of the preceding)

Metheg-ammah [c] bridle of metropolis, bridle of Ammah, bridle of the mother city, (i.e.: the jurisdiction of the metropolis), bridle of the dwarfs

Methusael man of God (El)

Methuselah man of God; extension of God; extremity of death; [man of a dart or a javelin?]

Meunim springs, people of Maon (same as *Mehunim*)

Mezahab offspring of the shining one; waters of gold

Miamin fortunate; on (or from) the right hand, i.e.: from the side of good luck

Mibhar choice, choicest; youth

Mibsam sweet odor, balsam

Mibzar a fortress, fortified, fortification

Micah (Michah) who (is) like (unto) Jah?

Micaiah who is like Jah?; (fuller form of *Micah*)

Micha (as above)

Michael who is like God? who is like unto God? [The Angel, also referred to as an archangel, symbolizes the aspect of consciousness that restores one onto the path towards the realization of Truth, particularly by the denial of the existence of evil].

Michaiah who is like Jah?; (same as *Micah*)

Michal who is like God? God is my king; brook; (possibly a shortened form of *Michael*)

Michmas [c] place of Chemosh, place of storage, a hidden place; treasured

Michmash [c] (another form of the preceding)

Michmethah [c] lurking place, [hiding place?]

Michri Jah possesses; a purchase price (in return for parents piety?); [precious?]

Michtam (the name of a particular kind of Psalm, meaning perhaps *golden* or *writing* or a Psalm of *attonement*)

Middin [c] extension (s), city of the judge

Midian contention; strife

Migdal-el [c] tower of God

Migdal-gad [c] tower of Gad (or fortune)

Migdol [c] tower

Migron [c] land slip, a precipice, threshing floor

Mijamin fortunate; on (or from) the right hand (i.e.: the side of good luck)

Mikloth rods, twigs, sticks, staves, lots

Mikneiah possession (or property) of Jah; Jah is zealous

Milalai Jah is elevated; [eloquent?]

Milcah counsel, queen

Milcom their king; (same as Molech, Malcham, or Malchan, the god of Ammonites) [Paradoxically, various scholars also offer different translations for some of those listed as "same"]

Miletus, Miletum red, scar-let; purest wool; {Gleamed from MBD}

Millo [c] filling, fulness, a mound, terrace, citadel; [the meaning of the word seems to have 'enlarged' with its use]

Miniamin fortunate; on the right hand; (longer form of *Mijamin*)

Minni allotted, appointed; distribution

Minnith [c] distribution, allotment, apportionment

Miphkad appointed place, place of meeting, enrolment or sum

Miriam fat, thick, strong; [rebellion? beloved one? Depending on the etymology chosen by a particular scholar]. (see *Mary*)

Mirma height; fraud, deceit

Misgab [c] the high land, height, secure height, refuge

Mishael who is what God is? Who belongs to God?

Misham swift, impetuous, haste, fame; cleansing

Misheal, Mishal [c] depression; prayer

Mishma fame; report; [rumor?]

Mishmannah strength, vigour; fat or fatness; tidbit

Mishraites drawn out, extended

Mispereth number or narrative; writing

Misrephoth-maim [c] place of lime burning at the water, burning (of) waters, burning of water hot-springs

Mithcah, Mithkah [c] sweet place; place of sweetness: [24th station of Israel from Egypt, 13th from Sinai]

Mithnite strength, firmness

Mithredath given by Mithra (i.e. sun), gift of (the god of light) Mithra

Mitylene [c] cleansing (?)

Mizar [c] little, small, smallness

Mizpah, Mizpeh [c] watchtower, a lookout

Mizpar writing; number or narrative; (see *Mispereth*)

Mizraim fortresses; [may have connections with Egypt, in which case it could suggest physicality and limitation]

Mizzah terror, joy; what is this?

Mnason mindful; reminding; remembering; inspiring; {Gleamed from MBD}

Moab water of a father, progeny of a father (possibly referring to a birth resulting from incest)

Moadiah festival of Jah, Jah is one who promises

Moladah [c] birth, origin

Molech, Moloch counsellor, king; [god of the Ammonites, also called *Milcon*, *Malcam* and *Malcan*, to whom human sacr-fices were offered].

Molid begetter

moon soul (the psyche, the intellect), particularly the *sub-conscious* (see *woman* and *water*)

Mordecai little man; dedicated to Mars; [worshiper of *Merodach*?] (From Akkadian: *Marduk*, the chief god of Babylon)

morning symbolizes fulfilment (see *evening*)

Moreh [c] teacher; archer

Moresheth-gath [c] the possession of Gath, possession of a wine press

Moriah [c] Jah provides, provided by Jah, Jah sees

Mosera [c] warning; chastisement; bond or fetter

Moseroth [c] bonds; (see preceding) [the 26th station in the wilderness, 15th from Sinai]

Moses drawer out, saved from the water, one drawn out;

mother & father 1. symbolize the *past* state of consciousness, (that which causes one to be that which one is today) 2. symbolize the state of consciousness before the feminine (*Is*) and the masculine (*Ra*) principles become unified into a spiritual entity by the awareness of the divine presence within (referred to as El).

mountain symbolizes the uplifted state of consciousness resulting from prayer, i.e. from the practice of the awareness of the Presence of God.

Moza origin, offspring, fountain, going forth, sunrise

Mozah [c] fountain, exit

multitude (s) (see *nations*)

Muppim obscurities

Mushi (God) has departed from me; drawn out, withdrawn

Muth-labben death of Ben, or of the son; [title of Psalm 9]

Myra [c] balsam; bitterness

Mysia beyond bounds, contemptible

N

Naam pleasant, charm, pleasantness

Naamah pleasant, lovely

Naaman pleasant, pleasantness

Naarah shoot, posterity; a girl

Naarai pleasantness of Jah, at-tendant of Jah; youthful, my youth

Naaran, Naarath [c] waterfall; boish; a girl; youthful

Naashon oracle; enchanter; serpent

Naason (Greek form of *Naashon*)

Nabal fool, foolish, reckless; projecting

Naboth prominence; deviation; [fruits? sprout?]

Nachon thrust, stroke; prepared
Nachor snorting
Nadab liberal, generous, willing
Nagge, (Naggai) (Greek form of *Nogah*)
Nahaliel valley (or torrent, or brook) of God; inheritance ofGod; (a station of the Israelites in the wilderness)
Nahal(l)al, Nahalol [c] drinking place (for flocks), a pasture
Naham he comforts, solace, consolation
Nahamani He comforts me, Jah has comforted, comforter
Naharai, Nahari snorting one), one who snores; [Arabic: *nihr* = intelligent]
Nahash oracle; serpent
Nahath lowness, descent, rest, quietness
Nahbi Jah is protection, consolation; hidden; faint hearted
Nahor piercer, slayer; [or another way of spelling *Nachor*]
Nahshon oracle; serpent; [same as *Naashon*]
Nahum (God is) compassionate; comforter; consolation
Nain [c] pasture; [also possible from Hebrew: *nîn* = offspring, or from *naîm* = pleasant].
Naioth [c] dwelling; habitations
name symbolizes the nature of that which is being named; all that comprises the sum-total of the character of an object and/or person thus designated.
name of the Lord symbolizes the nature of the indwelling Christ
Naomi pleasant, my sweetness or delight, my pleasantness
Naphish, Nephish wealth; numerous; cheerful; refreshed; animated; breathing; rational; [refers to the breath of life at conscious and unconscious level]
Naphtali wrestling, my wrestling
Naphtuhim [inhabitants of central Egypt] they who are of Ptah; bowmen(?)
Narcissus flower causing lethargy; benumbing
Nathan (God) has given, giver; gift
Nathan-melech the king is giver, gift of the king, the king

has given

Nathanael gift of God, God has given

nation (s) symbolizes the thoughts from which we have built our mental reality, thus: the state of mental consciousness; (see *hosts, multitudes*)

Naum comfort; (Greek form of *Nahum*)

Nazareth [c] branch; set apart; [the symbolic meaning is that which has its being *in* but not *of* the world].

Nazarite (one) separated, devoted, consecrated; [the appellation of one who by a vow refrains from certain things for a longer or shorter time]

Neah [c] the settlement; of a slope

Neapolis new city

Neariah Jah drives away; servant (or attendant) of Jah, the boy (that is, servant) of Jah, armor bearer

Nebai marrowy, projection; fruitful, my fruit

Nebaioth, Nebajoth husbandry; high places; [pertaining to *Nabu*, a Babylonian god, son of Marduk? Also note Arabic: *nabawat* = lofty places, eminences]

Neballat [c] hard, firm

Nebat (God) has looked, he (that is God) has seen, look, cultivation, aspect

Nebo [c] height; a lofty place; [Babylonian god *Nabu*, son of Marduk. Also planet Mercury]

Nebuchadnezzar Nebo protect the crown; may (the god) Nabu protect the son, may Nabu protect the boundary. [Symbolic meaning might be derived from the fact that Nebuchadnezzar, the king of Babylon, invaded Judah, captured and destroyed Jerusalem and the temple, carried the inhabitants to Babylon, set up a golden image in the plain of Dura, threw young men into a fiery furnace, became proud.... yet, ultimately praised God! I might suggest that Nebuchadnezzar is symbolic of you and me, of everyone....]

Nebushasban Nebo (will) save me; [*Nebo* and *Nebu* are the same]

Nebuzar-adan Nebo gives (or has given) posterity (or offspring)

Necho, Nechoh conquered; smitten; lame

Nedabiah Jah is willing, (or liberal or generous); [Jah is bountiful?]

Neginah, Neginoth [music of a kind of stringed instrument, or the musical instrument itself]

Nehalamite dreamer, dreamed

Nehemiah Jah is comfort, Jah comforts (of has comforted)

Nehiloth name of a music choir, inheritance; flutes; (Psalm 5, title)

Nehum comfort, comforted, consolation

Nehushta basis, ground, support; bronze, serpent, of bronze (denoting strength)

Nehushtan brazen serpent; brazen, bronze serpent idol

Neiel [c] dwelling of God; moved by God; God is pleasant

Nekeb [c] the hollow, cavern, pass, a narrow pass

Nekoda a herdsman; moor hen; dotted, speckled

Nemuel God is spreading; [same as *Jemuel*?]

Nepheg sprout; [Hebrew: *nepeg* = slow, sluggish]

Nephish (see *Naphish*)

Nephishesim expansions; inspiring or refreshing breaths

Nephthalim (Greek form of *Naphtali*)

Nephtoah opened, opening

Nephusim expansions; refreshing breaths

Nephishesim (as above)

Ner light, a lamp; shining

Nereus god of water

Nergal lion; fierace warrior; [The war god of the men of Cuth. Also planet Mars]

Nergal-sharezer Nergal protect the king

Neri (Greek form of *Neriah*)

Neriah Jah is light (of a lamp), lamp of Jah, Jah is my lamp

Nethaneel God gives, gift of God, God has given; (same as *Nathanael*)

Nethaniah Jah gives, whom Jah gave, Jah has given

Nethinims the given ones, dedicated; the appointed
Netophah [c] resin-dropping, dripping
Neziah pre-eminent, illustrious, excellent
Nezib [c] plantation; garrison; pillar
Nibhaz barker; pulsating; striking; [An idol of the Avites, in the form of a dog]
Nibshan [c] fertile ground; [level?], the furnace
Nicanor conqueror, victorious
Nicodemus victor over the people; innocent blood
Nicolas conqueror of the people; (The deeds of the *Nicolaitanes* are condemned without being mentioned)
Nicopolis [c] city of victory
Niger black
night often symbolizes the subconscious mind
Nimrah [c] flowing water, limpid (water); (see *Beth-nimrah*)
Nimrim [c] limpid waters, flowing streams, clear waters; [leopards?]
Nimrod valiant, strong
Nimshi Jah reveals; [discloser?], ichneumon: (Egyptian ichneumon is a weasel-like animal, or a mongoose)
Nineveh [c] dwelling of Ninus; growing vigor; exterior growth; handsome; agreeable; [The name was associated with "fish", an allusion to the river goddess Nina, whose emblem was a fish].
Nisan new day; newness; sparking; blooming; month of flowers or green ears; opening or beginning (from Akkadian: *nisannu*) [The first month of the Hebrew religious year – called *Abib* in the Books of Moses – beginning with thenew moon of March or April. It is also the name of the Babylonian god of "spring"]
Nisroch eagle, hawk; [An Assyrian idol with a temple in Nineveh; it had a human form with an eagle's head]
No [c] (from *nw.t* or *niwt*, meaning: city or village (of Amon); [Same as Thebes, a capital of Upper Egypt, chief seat of the worship of Amon].

Noadiah Jah assembles, whom Jah meets, Jah has met (me), Jah has manifested himself

Noah 1. rest, comfort, cheer; (Symbolizes the spiritual self; also everyone who has faith in his intuition i.e. his spiritual self). 2. flattery; wandering; a quivering, trembling; (Numbers 26:33)

Noah's sons Noah and his sons: Shem, Ham and Japheth symbolize the fourfold nature of man, i.e. the physical, intellectual, and the emotional – Noah representing the spiritual nature himself. (see horses)

Nob[c] height; high place

Nobah a barking, a dog's bark; prominent

Nod (land of) [c] wandering, flight, banishment; [symbolizes belief in the negative power]

Nodab liberal, willing; nobility, noble

Noe (Greek form of *Noah*)

Nogah shining, brightness, splendor; watering place

Nohah rest, quiet

noise symbolizes the abundance of (uncontrolled) thoughts flooding our consciousness.

Non continuation; fish, (same as *Nun*)

Noph [c] (same as *Memphis* or *Moph*)

Nophah [c] height; windy

North (Hebrew: *saphôn*) symbolizes that which is concealed; (see *east*)

number of the beast: 666, i.e. abortive work; work without fulfilment; total failure or inability to realize the Presence of God. (see *six*)

Nun fish; continuation; spread-ing abroad; prolific; pesterity.

O

oak trees (**terebinths**) invariably symbolize spiritual
strength [in Hebrew oak tree is *elah,* thus sharing the
root of both *El* and *Jah*, implying divine intervention]
Obadiah servant (or worshiper) of Jah
Obal bare; barren; stripped.
Obed worshiping (God), serving, servant or server
Obed-edom servant of Edom; serving Edom
Obil driver, leader; camel-keeper (or -driver)
Oboth [c] bottles (of skin), water-skins; hollows; [Astation
of Israel, east of Edom]
Ocran trouble, troublesome, troubler, affliction
Oded aiding; restorer; [setting up?]
Og long necked; giant; [circle?]
Ohad powerful, might
Ohel family, race, tent
Oholah (see Aholah)
oil, ointment are symbols of praise and thanksgiving
O Jacob an abbreviation for *Oh God of Jacob*
olive leaf (or branch) symbolizes accomplishment.
olive trees (two) symbolize the *Is* and *Ra*, i.e. the female
and the male principles of human nature. [In the
Revelation of John the *two olive trees* are pictured on
either side of the candlestick that symbolizes the *El,*
the unifying principle. (see *Israel*)]
Olivet olives, of a place (or grove) of olives, [Also a ridge
of mountains, the Mount of Olives] (mountains always
signify raised consciousness)
Olympas Elysian, heavenly
Omar talkative, word, song, praise, the speaking one;
mountaineer
Omega [the last letter of Greek alphabet (as Alpha is the
first)]

O

Omri Jah apportions; the worshiper, [probably from Arabic root: *'mr* meaning to *thrive* or *live long*]

On [c] (place) the sun, house of the sun; [Capital of Lower Egypt. Also called Heliopolis, as well as Beth-shemesh, i.e.: *house of the sun*]

On (person) vigor, strength, wealth, power

Onam wealthy, strong, vigorous

Onan strong, wealthy, vigorous

Onesimus profitable, useful

Onesiphorus bringing (or bringer of) profit, carrier of profit, profit bearing

Ono [c] strong, vigorous

Ophel [c] the high place, a hill, knoll, swelling, lump

Ophir fat, rich

Ophni [c] the high place; man of the hill

Ophrah [c] faun, hind, young hart, stag

Oreb raven, bustard

Oren pine-tree, a species of fir or cedar tree; laurel; strength

Orion strong, insolent one, fool, stupid one, impudent, defiant: [derived from *kesîl*, the Hebrew designation for a constellation of stars named for the mighty *Hunter* in Greek mythology]

Ornan freeman, aristocrat, lord, strong; (also called *Araunah*)

Orpah stubborn, youthful freshness, neck (implying stiff neck, i.e.: stubborn; [hind?]

Osee (Greek name for *Hosea*)

Oshea God saves, Jah is salvation, may Jah save

Othni Jah is force; [powerful?] (see the following)

Othniel God is force, powerful man of God

Ozem strength, hot-tempered

Ozias (Greek form of Uzziah: *Jah is strong*)

Ozni Jah hears, Jah gives ear; hearing, my ear

P

Paarai revelation of Jah; [devoted to Peor?]
Padan [c] plain
Padan-aram [c] the plain of Aram; the plain of Syria
Padon deliverance, redemption, ransom
Pagiel God meets, God has entreated (or met), intervention of God, [destiny of God?]
Pahath-moab prefect (or governor) of Moab
Pai yawning deep, groaning; (same as *Pau*)
Palal a judge, God has judged (or decided),
Palestina emigration; [land of strangers?]
Pallu, Phallu distinguished, wonderful, excelling
palm (tree) symbolizes those that bear witness to the Truth; [often referred to as martyrs].
palms (of hands) particularly the left hand, may symbolize destiny
Palti my salvation, Jah delivers, deliverance of Jah, He (that is God) delivered me
Paltiel, Phaltiel God is salvation, God delivers, deliverance of God, God has delivered
Paltite a descendant of Palti
Pamphylia a mixture of people
Pannag [c] sweet; [could also be come kind of grain product] (also called *Piggi*)
Parah [c] heifer, young cow; the wild place
Paran [c] full of caverns; cavernous
Parbar [c] open summer house; open apartment
Parmashta first, greatest, superior
Parmenas standing firm, persistent
Parnach agile, swift; delight oneself; to live delicately; to weaken with tenderness
Parosh, Pharosh fleeing, fugitive
Parshandatha given to question, inquisitive; (from Old

Persian)

Parthians horsemen (?)

Paruah increase, blooming, flourishing, joyous, happy

Parvaim [an unknown gold region] eastern; original; primal prior; anterior; virgin purity; pure virgin gold; {Gleamed from MBD}

Pasach limping; divider

Pas-dammim [c] extremity of the flowings; (shortened from *Ephes-dammim*)

Paseah, Phaseah limping, lame, one who limps

Pashur free; prosperity round about; [Egyptian: *Psh Hr* = portion of Horus]

Passover passing over, as in over of stream or obstruction; overcoming; sparing; delivering.

pastures particularly *green* pastures, symbolize a sating of our needs. In a way, they are the spiritual ideas upon which we feed our thoughts.

Patara [c] trampled, contempt

Pathros the south (or southern) land, (i.e.: Upper Egypt or Thebaid, as distinguished from Mazor, Lower Egypt)

Patharusim inhabitants of the above

Patmos mortal; (A sterile island in the Ægean sea) Symbolizes physical or mortal (state of) consciousness

patriarch head of the father's house

Pathrobas according to the father; patrimony

Pau [c] crying out; screaming; lowing; blowing; (older form of *Pai*)

Paul, Paulus little or small; (the title assumed by Saul: *little one*)

Pedahel God delivers, God (has) redeemed (or delivered)

Pedahzur the rock delivers, the Rock (has) redeemed

Pedaiah Jah delivers, whom Jah (has) redeemed (or delivered)

Pekah (God) has opened (the eyes), watchfulness, open-eyed, opening

Pekahiah Jah has opened (the eyes), Jah watches, whose

eyes Jah opened

Pekod [c] visitation; [a symbolic name for *Chaldea*]

Pelaiah Jah is distinguished, whom Jah made distinguished, Jah is marvelous (or wonderful), Jah has performed a miracle

Pelaliah Jah judges, whom Jah judged, Jah intervened

Pelatiah Jah delivers, whom Jah delivered, Jah has delivered

Peleg division, canal

Pelet (God) has set free, deliverance, rescue, escape, liberation

Peleth flight, haste, swiftness, swift (of a horse)

Pelethites runners; (see preceding?)

Peniel [c] the face of God

Peninnah coral; [or from Arabic: one with rich (or beautiful) hair]

Pentecost fiftieth; (Feast on 50th day after Passover, i.e. reaping and harvest of grain).

Penuel [c] face of God; (old form of *Peniel*)

people symbolize thoughts; thoughts "populate" our minds, inhabit the "cites" of our consciousness. (see *men*)

Peor opening; point; [referred to as: 1. A mountain in Moab; 2. The Moabite god of uncleanness]

Perazim breaches, gasps; (compare *Baal-parazim*)

Peres to divide, part, divided

Peresh separate, distinction; dung

Perez bursting through; breach

Perez uzza(h) [c] the breach of Uzzah (of Strength of Jah)

Perga [c] very earthly; physical; (The capital of Pamphylia which had a famous temple of Diana or Artemis)

Pergamos [c] acropolis, or citadel, or fortress; (The city housed the famous temple of *Esculapius* who was represented under the figure of a serpent)

Perida separation, isolation, a recluse, single, unique

Perizzites belonging to a village, villagers

Persia [one called Elam] see Elam

Persis Persian
Peruda separation, isolation; (same as *Perida*)
Peter a stone, a rock; unyielding
Pethahiah Jah opens (the womb), whom Jah looses
Pethor [c] extension
Pethuel God delivers; youth of God, [a youth belonging to God? God's opening?]
Peulthai Jah works, deed of Jah, recompense (or reward) of Jah
Phalec (Greek form of *Peleg*)
Phallu (English spelling of *Pallu*)
Phalti (same as *Palti*)
Phaltiel (same as *Paltiel*)
Phanuel (Greek form of *Penuel*)
Pharaoh the great house (or palace), the sun; [the king of Egypt symbolizes the "lower self" often referred to as the ego]
Pharaoh-hophra priest of the sun
Pharaoh-nechhoh (or **-necho**) stricken with the sun, lame
Phares (Greek form of *Pharez*)
Pharez, Perez breaking forth, breach
Pharisees separate, the separated, separate ones; [They tended to interpret the letter and not the spirit of the law. In this sense they could be compared to today's 'fundamentalists']
Pharosh (see *Paroch*)
Pharpar swift, haste
Phaseah (see *Paseah*)
Phebe radiant, pure, bright; moon
Phenice date palm, palm tree
Phenicia land of palms; [or from Greek *phoinix*: purple red, purple or crimson]
Phibeseth [c] the cat goddess Basht; (a capital city in Lower Egypt).
Phichol great, strong, tamarisk; [attentive?]
Philadelphia brotherly love

Philemon affectionate, loving
Philetus beloved, worthy of love
Philip a lover (or fond) of horses
Philippi [c] city of Philip (of lover of horses)
Phiilistia migration; [the land of the Philistines]
Philistim wanderers, migrants; transitory
Philistines (as preceding)
Philologus fond of learning, lover of words; talkative
Phinehas oracle; serpent's mouth; the Nubian
Phlegon burning, zealous
Phœbe (see Phebe)
Phurah beauty; [branch?]
Phut, Put bow
Phuvah, Pua utterance; mouth; madder (dyer's red)
Phygellus little fugitive
phylactery aguard, charm; [A small leather box containing
    slips of vellum inscribed with Hebrew texts, worn by
    Jews as a reminder to keep the Law. "To make broad
    phylacteries" means to make an ostentatious display of
    one's righteousness]. {Gleaned from The Concise
    Oxford Dictionary of Current English. Oxford
    University Press 1964.}
Pibeseth (see *Phibeseth*)
Pi-hahiroth [c] place of meadows; where sedge grows;
    house of (the Egyptian deity) Hrt; [Israel's last
    stopping place before crossing the Red Sea]
Pilate armed with a javelin, a spear
Pildash flame of fire; spider; [steel?]
Pileha harelip, having a cleft in lower lip; worship;
    millstone; [plowman?]
Piltai (Jah is) deliverance, Jah causes to escape, whom Jah
    delivers
Pinon ore pit; darkness
Piram wild, roving; (like a) wild ass, onager
Pirathon peak, top, leader, height

Pisgah peak, point, cleft; a part, boundary

Pisidia tanacious; clining;

Pison (Pishon) freely flowing; [One of the four rivers of Eden that symbolize the fourfold nature of man: *Pison*, the spiritual nature, *Gihon* the emotional, *Hiddekel* symbolizes the intellect and *Euphrates* the body, the physical consciousness. Note that the river is one until it leaves Eden, only then it divides into four branches].

Pispah expansion

pit symbolizes the deeper recesses of one's subconscious mind; (see *the bottomless pit*)

Pithom [c] narrow pass; house (or temple) of (the Egyptian god) Atum

Pithon opened; harmless; [simple?]

place symbolizes a state of consciousness, as does a city, a room or anywhere where we pause at any moment of our journey to God realization.

plagues symbolize the destructive consequences of negative thoughts, negative traits of character. They are the result of the *'beast'* controlling our awareness. (see *locust*)

plain (the) symbolizes fears, doubts, negative attitudes.

Pleiades [(coming at) the sailing season?] [It is a cluster of seven stars, known in Hebrew as *kîmâ*, from *kûm*, meaning: to accumulate].

Pochereth-harrebaim binder (of the gazelles), pit ofgazelles, gazelle hunter,

Pollux (see *Castor*)

poor (in spirit) invariably refers to being humble. The 'scarcity' refers to the diminution of one's ego so that the Higher Self, the *El*, might take over.

Pontius belonging to the sea

Pontius mariner, belonging to the sea

Pontus sea; deep

Poratha giving much, liberal; [having many chariots?]

Porcius Festus swinish-joyful: a joyful pig

Potiphar belonging to the sun, the one whom the (sun god) Ra has given, the one sent by Ra (also spelt Re)

Poti-pherah (same as preceding)

prayer symbolizes a raising or the process of raising one's consciousness, although in Coptic writings the word is used in a literal sense and thus discouraged (see *mountain*); {See Stanislaw Kapuscinski's *Key to Immortality*, a Commentary on the *Gospel According to Thomas* logion 14, Smashwords 2010}

prince (of God) symbolizes or is symbolized by *Israel*. The title describes a soul that realized (is fully aware of) its Divine nature.

prince (of the world) symbolizes him who is subject to the limitations of carnal mind.

Prisca, Priscilla ancient, revered little woman

Promised Land symbolizes the state of consciousness in which we (can) achieve Self-realization, i.e. the conscious awareness of the indwelling Christ, the I AM. [It is a subjective experience that each one must find for oneself].

Prochorus he that presides over a choir, leader of dancers

prophets had been essentially teachers; their prophecies (including promises) had been intended towards the spiritual development of a soul. In this sense they are as pertinent today as they were in their day.

Ptolemais [c] warlike

Pua (see *Phuvah*)

Puah 1. lass, girls, splendor; 2. madder (dye)

Publius common

Pudens shamefaced, modest, bashful

Pul strong

Punon [c] ore-pit; darkness; [see Pinon] [The 35th station from Egypt, 24th from Sinai]

Pur part; lot, portion

Purim lots (same as *Pur*)

Put (see *Phut*)
Puteoli [c] (little) wells, fountains, craters, sulfur springs
Putiel God enlightens, he whom God has given, the one
  given by God.
Pygarg species of an antelpe

Q

Quartus the fourth
queen of the south symbol-izes a soul capable of making a
  conscious demonstration, i.e. of obtaining results from
  prayers; ["queen" being feminine, symbolizes the soul
  (including the *subconscious*), even as king has (or
  should have) control over the *conscious* mind. Note
  that a demonstration is always preceded by the
  actionof the subconscious]
quicken to keep, preserve or give life.

R

Raamah thunder, trembling; mane of a horse; [or from
  Arabic: *raghama*: to constrain, humiliate]
Raamiah Jah causes trembling, trembling of Jah, Jah has
  shaken
Raamses [c] son of the sun, he whom (the sun god) Ra has
  begotten
Rabbah, Rabbath [c] great or large (city), capitol city
Rabbi a great man, (my) teacher, (my) master, my great
  one
Rabbith [c] the great place; populous, numerous (city)
Rabboni my rabbi, my master, my teacher
Rab-mag head of Magi; most exalted; (a title of a high

office)

Rab-saris head of eunuchs, chief eunuch; confidant or a court official

Rab-shakeh head (chief) of the cup bearers, the chief cup-bearer

Raca vein, empty, fool; [it refers to the absence of Spirit]

Rachab (Greek form of *Rahab*)

Rachal [c] traffic, place of traffic, market, trade, commerce

Rachel a lamb, ewe

Raddai Jah subdues (or rules); subduing

Ragau (Greek form of *Reubem*)

Raguel Jah is friend, friend of God; (same as *Reuel*)

Rahab (1). storm, arrogancy, one who rages, tumult, violence; [a symbolic name for Egypt used in Psalms and Isaiah].

Rahab, Rachab (2). breadth, broad, wide, extended

Raham he has shown compassion, mercy, pity, love

Rahel (see *Rachel*)

rainbow symbolizes the etheric (or ethereal) body, the aura; [a symbol similar to the many-colored coat of Joseph]. The etheric body is colored in accordance with our habitual thoughts.

Rakem friendship; variegated, variegation; multihued

Rakkath [c] bank, shore, narrow place; flowing

Rakkon [c] well watered; (also given as same as *Rakkath*)

Ram high, exalted

Rama, Ramah [c] height; high place

Ramath [c] (same as preceding)

Ramathaim [c] double high place, twin heights

Ramath-lehi [c] high place hill) of the jaw bone; height of Lehi

Ramath-mizpeh [c] place of watchtower, lookout height, height of Mizpeh

Rameses [c](see *Raamses*)

Ramiah Jah is high, Jah is exalted

Ramoth [c] heights, high places

Ramoth-gilead [c] height of Gilead

Rapha he (God) has healed, (God) heals; fearful; [giant?]

Raphael God heals, God has healed, God is helping me; (in apocryphal and pseudepigraphic literature). Raphael symbolizes the conviction of the Presence of God, which normally results in a healing process.

Raphu healed, cured

Raven symbolizes negative (dark) thoughts.

Reaiah Jah sees, Jah has seen

Reba sprout, offspring; fourth, a fourth part

Rebecca, Rebekah flattering; a noose, loop of rope, to tie, bind

Rechab horseman, charioteer, rider; companionship

Rechah [c] declivity; soft place; [side?]

red The colour red symbolizes emotions or the emotional nature (thus: the red horse, the great red dragon, the scarlet woman, etc.)

Red Sea (the crossing of the-) This is a combination of the color red and the sea. It symbolizes a great change in both: emotions and mindset.

Reelaiah Jah causes trembling, trembling caused by Jah, Jah has shaken

Regem friendship, association; friend

Regem-melech friend of the king

Rehabiah Jah is a widener, Jah enlarges, Jah has enlarged

Rehob [c] street, open space, plaza, wide street, width

Rehoboam freer of the people,who enlarges the people, the people have been enlarged, the divine kinsman has enlarged

Rehoboth [c] enlargement, roominess, open spaces (streets or places)

Rehum compassionated (by God), God has shown mercy; pity, mercy, merciful

Rei Jah is a friend; friendly

Rekem (same as *Rakem*)

Remaliah Jah increases, whom Jah adorned, soothsayer of

Jah

Remeth [c] height, a high place

Remmon [c] (see *Rimmon*)

Remmon-methoar pomegranate stretching (to Neah)

Remphan [An idol (star god) worshipped by Israel in the wilderness, perhaps same as *Chiun*]

Rephael God is healer, whom God healed, God has healed; pleasant, agreeable

Rephah healing, support; riches, easy life

Rephaiah Jah heals (or cures), whom Jah healed, Jah has healed

Rephaim(s) strong; giants

Rephidim plains, expanses, stretches; supports; [A station of Israel where Moses struck a rock in Horeb, and supplied water]

Resen [c] fortress; bridle

Resheph flame; haste

resurrection symbolizes the metamorphosis of man's consciousness from sensual to spiritual.

Reu friendship, friend; (short for *Reuel*)

Reuben behold a son

Reuel God is friend; friend of God

Reumah pearl, coral; exalted

Rezeph [c] stronghold; a stone

Rezia Jah is pleasing; delight, pleasant

Rezin dominion; firm; brook; pleasant

Rezon prince, noble, weighty, dignitary; lean

Rhegium [c] breach

Rhesa principle, chief; (and ancestor of Jesus)

Rhoda a rose, a rose bush

Rhodes rose, roses

Ribai Jah judges (or contends or strives); contentious

Riblah [c] bare place; fertility [from Arabic: *rabala* = to multiply] (also see *Diblath*)

right hand symbolizes the executive power, the ability and the authority to get 'things' done. [The Hebrews also referred to the right hand (or side) as the fortunate one]

righteousness symbolizes right thinking. [Hebrew *tsaddiq, yashar, tsadaq* are all variously translated as righteous, just, upright, right, to be right]

Rimmon [c] pomegranate

Rimmon-parez [c] pomegran-ate of the breach; (The 15th station of Israel from Egypt, 4th from Sinai)

Rinnah a shout, cry, a ringing cry (as an object of joy); strength

Riphath disheartened; scattered; [Some scholars claim that Riphath and his descendants marched across the Richaen i.e. the Carpathian Mountains, into the farthest regions of Europe].

Rissah [c] a ruin, heap of ruins; dew or rain, sprinkling; [The 17th station of Israel from Egypt, 6th from Sinai]

Rithmah (place of the) broom, broom plant; [The 14th station of Israel form Egypt, 3rd from Sinai]

river (a directional flow) symbolizes a *change* in consciousness. *Crossing the water* demonstrates a victory over oneself. [Note: a prefix *hi* or *hai* (lively) is used for running]

Rizpah hot coal (or stone), glowing coals; variegated

Roboam (Greek form of *Rehoboam*)

rock symbolizes a state of consciousness built upon right-thinking. It is the symbol of the Christ Truth, that which is immutable, eternal. Thus the Temple of Solomon [a state of consciousness wherein peaceprevails] is built upon a rock.

rod symbolizes: 1. a sceptre, [a badge of office, a symbol of power]; 2. an offshoot or branch of a family or tribe; that which ensues from one's efforts. (see *son*)

Rogelim [c] fullers' place, spies, fullers

Rohgah outcry, alarm

Romamti–ezer highest help, I have exalted help, I have gloried in help

Rosh head or chief
ruby (the stone) symbolizes Divine Love
Rufus red
Ruhamah she has received compassion, pitied,
    compassionated; [A symbolic name of Israel].
Rumah [c] height, high place
Ruth friendship

S

Sabachthani hast thou forsaken me? (*Eli! Eli! lama
    sabachthani?*)
Sabaoth hosts, armies; [The Lord of hosts symbolizes a
    state of consciousness that ultimately rules over all our
    thoughts and emotions, i.e.: over our psyche or soul.
    This power within is variously referred to as the
    Christ, the I AM, the El, or the Higher Self]. (see
    hosts)
Sabbath the seventh; rest, cessation, to cease; [Sabbath
    (number seven) symbolizes the fulfilment. In the
    practical sense, we are taught that we must *cease* any
    and all *conscious* activity (including that which is
    normally regarded as prayer) before the *subconscious*
    (soul) has a chance to do its work. Sometimes we
    must "just be". Compare: "Be still, and know that I am
    God: (Psalm 46:10)].
Sabta(h) orbit, curcuit; determining motion; a turn;
    course of action; stiking; rock; strokeSabtecha(h)
    determined movement; extreme oppression,
    enchaining; compressive surroudings, great stroke;
    [as Sabta (above) but greately intensified]
Sacar hired, hire, reward (of God), wages
sackcloth a rough cloth originally made of goats' hair worn
    as a symbol of penitence and/or of mourning. The

wearing of sackcloth was often accompanied by the sprinkling ashes on one's head.

Sadducee [A Jewish sect (named after Zadok) who denied the resurrection, the existence of angels and spirits (from Hebrew: *sadaq* or from *Zadoc* meaning: 'to be righteous').

Sadoc just, righteous; (Greek form of *Zadoc*)

saints symbolize the redeemed traits of character, and as such form an indestructible 'component' of our spiritual consciousness.

Sala, Salah (Greek form of *Shelah*)

Salamis [c] (possibly: fertility)

Salathiel (Greek form of *Shealtiel*)

Salchah, Salcah [c] wander-ing; road

Salem [c] summit, whole, perfect, complete; peaceful, peace, safe; [As the city of Melchizedek, it symbolizes a state of consciousness equivalent to Jerusalem].

Salim [c] (Greek form of *Salem*)

Sallai rejecter; exaltation; [(God) compensated? Arabic: *sala'a* = pay promptly].

Sallu 1. contempt, rejection, (see preceding); 2. weighed, dear

Salma strength, firmness, cover

Salmon (Psalm 68:14): terrace, ascent; shady, cover; (see *Zalmon*)

Salmone agitated; commotion

Salome perfect, peace, (from Hebrew *shalôm* = wellbeing)

Salu miserable, unfortunate; restored; (see *Sallu, Sallai*) [MBD offers: lifted up; weighed; judged; exalted]

salvation symbolizes the full realization of Oneness with God. Also the Power within (*El*) which brings about such a state of consciousness. {For those interested I recommend my essays *Sanctifying* and *Salvation* in BEYOND RELIGION I, Inhousepress '98, '01, 2002; Smshwords 2010]}

Samaria [c] lookout, watch, guard, (Greek equivalent of

Shomron meaning: guard).

Samgar-nebo be gracious, gracious interpreter; graciousness of Nebo;　[from Sumarian shumgir-Nabu?　Nebo is a Babylonian or Chaldean god symbolizing psychic powers], also: sword of Mercury (symbolizing intellect]

Samlah garment, abode; [Arabic *shaml* = unity, oneness]

Samos [noted for its worship of the Roman queen of gods Juno, the sister and wife of Jupiter]

Samson like the sun, little sun, solar; distinguished, strong; [other suggested meanings: fat, robust or destroyer]

Samuel heard of God, God has heard, name of God, His name is El

Sanballat Sin (the moon-god) gives (or has given) life; (see *moon*)

Sansannah [c] instruction (see *Kirjath-senneh*); palm branch, palm panicle

Saph preserver; threshold

Saphir [c] beautiful, pleasant, thorny, (see *Shamir*)

Sapphira (Greek feminine form of the preceding)

sapphire [This deep-blue stone also called Lapis Lazuli symbolizes the Divine Truth]

Sara, Sarah princess, noble woman

Sarai Jah is prince;　(contentious?)　[The original name and/or older spelling of Sarah, wife of Abraham]

Saraph burning (one) or serpent

Sardis [c] precious stone, prince of joy [sardius = ruby]

Sarepta [c] (Greek form of *Zarephath*)

Sargon The king is legitimate, (God) appoints the king

Sarid [c] refuge; survivor

Saron (Greek form of *Sharon*)

Sarsechim chief of the eunuchs

Saruch (Greek form of *Serug*)

satan adversary, the hater, accuser

Saul, Shaul asked (of God) or lent (to God), asked for

scarlet woman (of Babylon) symbolizes the emotional

nature of soul in its negative aspects.

Sceva left-handed

scorpion (torment of) symbolizes a mental and/or spiritual paralysis, i.e. a loss of hope, an affirmation of belief in one's limitations.

sea (s) symbolizes the mental aspect of human nature, particularly the subconsciousness; (see *moon, waters*)

Seba dirinking to excess; drunken; intoxicated; vital fluid; condensaations; sap; turning; reeling

Sebat [rest?] [The 11th month of Jewish religious year, beginning with the new moon of January or February]

Scacah [c] enclosure, inclosure, barricade, thicket, cover

Sechu [c] watchplace, watchtower, lookout

secret place symbolizes a condition of raised consciousness; (see *chamber*)

Secundus second

Segub (God is) exalted, elevated; might, protection

Seir rough, wooded, hairy, shaggy; (i.e.: covered with brushwood)

Seirath [c] forested, (the) wooded, well-wooded; (see *Seir*)

Sela [c] (the) rock or cliff; fortress

Selah tranquil; secure; silence; [a musical direction in Psalms]

Sela-hammahlekoth rock of (the) separations (or divisions or smoothness); rock of escapes

Seled exultation, leaping for joy; [burning?]

Seleucia [c] troubled; aflicted

Sem (Greek form of *Shem*)

Semachiah Jah supports, whom Jah sustains, Jah has sustained

Semei (Greek form of *Shimei*)

Senaah [c] (see *Hassenaah*)

Seneh pointed rock; crag, thorn, thorn-bush

Senir peak or snowy mountain; coat of mail

Sennacherib Sin (the moon) multiplies brethren; may (the god) Sin increase my brothers; Sin has replaced the (lost) brothers; (see *moon*)

Senuah (see *Hasenuah*)

Seorim fear, distress; barley

Sephar a numbering; spiritual travail; meditation; remembering; writing; scroll; sacred writing

Sepharad boundary; limit; divided number; severed

Sepharvaim [c] dual meditations; two inscriptions; two books or letters; two scribes; [The city's inhabitants, the Sepharvites, were apparently accustomed to burning their children in the fire to Adram-melech and Anammelech, their gods. I would suggest that such myths are a symbolic description of the act of cleansing their negative thoughts, the dross of their minds] (see *fire, children*)

Serah, Sarah extension, abundance

Seraiah Jah is prince (or ruler), Jah contends (or rules)

Seraphim burning, noble; burning ones; [Symbolic beings seen in vision]

Sered escape, deliverance; fear, to be terrified

serpent usually symbolizes limitation, the easy way. It can also stand for our carnal mind i.e.: our physical consciousness. [It should be noted that a *snake* can symbolize the emotional nature which, when redeemed (conquered) becomes an *eagle*]. Paradoxically, in the Gnostic literature, the serpent is a symbol for divine wisdom.

Serug strength, firmness; shoot; tendril

Seth, Sheth appointed, substitute, compensation, sprout

Sethur hidden (by God), secreted

seven number seven symbolizes (i.e.: is indicative of) individual perfection and fulfilment.

seven heads of the *dragon*: symbolize the opposite of individual perfection, i.e.: the seven principle negative traits of character. [Compare: seven deadly sins].

Shaalabbin [c] jackals; earth of foxes, foxes

Shaalbim (same as preceding)

Shaaph union, friendship; balsam; [anger?]
Sha(a)raim [c] double cleft; two gates
Shaashgaz [beauty's servant?]
Shabbethai born on the Sabbath
Shachia fame of Jah, Jah looks out, Jah has hedged about; lustful
shadow of death (the land of the…) symbolizes physical consciousness. Only Spirit has substance, all else is imaginary, transient, thus 'a shadow'. Note that *shadow* can also symbolize 'protection'.
Shadrach, M. & A. Shadrach (Hananiah: *God is gracious*), **Meshach** (Michael: *where is God?*) and **Abednego**: (*servant of light*) symbolize the emotional, physical and intellectual nature. (N.B.: the 'fourth man' represents the spiritual nature, the true Self.) Compare: the four horseman in the Book of Revelation. Also, Noah and his three sons.
Shage wandering, wanderer, erring; [presumably wandering away from the true path]
Shahar (see *Aijeleth Shahar*)
Shaharaim double dawn, two dawns, (born at the hour of) dawn
Shahazimah [c] high place, heights, lofty places
Shalem [c] peace, summit; safe, perfect
Shalim jackal, foxes; [Hebrew *sha'alîm* = hollow hands?]
Shalisha third ground; a third part
Shallecheth casting out; felling. [The gates to the temple symbolize new understanding or the processes of acquiring new understanding within one's consciousness]
Shallum recompenser or recompensed, retribution, restoration; recompensed (by God) for loss of a previous child
Shallun restored; completed; prosperous; peaceful; restitution
Shalmai (Jah is) well-being, Jah is peace, peaceful; Jah is

recompenser

Shalman fire worshiper; [a reminder that fire symbolizes a cleansing or purifying process. Shalman being an Assyrian king, the purification would refer to the mental or intellectual consciousness]

Shalmaneser fire worshiper; Shalman is chief (or superior); Shalman be propitious; modesty opposed to vehemence; (An Assyrian king who invaded Israel and carried off Hoshea and the ten tribes to Assyria). (see above)

Shama he hears, he (God) has heard, God hears, hearer; obedient

Shamariah (see *Shemariah*)

Shamed destroyer, destruction

Shamer keeper, preserver, (God is) a keeper, guard

Shamgar (the god) Shimike has given; cupbearer, fleer; [destroyer?]

Shamhuth fame, renown; (born at the time of a) horrible event, 'appallment' (referring to a terrible event at the time of birth), [notoriety?]

Shamir [c] thorn hedge (or bush), a thorn or emery, flint; approved

Shamma, Shammah fame, renown; desert; horror; [(God) has heard?]

Shammai celebrated; wasted; [Jah has heard?]

Shammoth fame, renwn; deserts; horror

Shammua, Shammuah heard (by God); famous

Shamsherai heroic

Shapham youthful, vigorous; bald; [rock badger?]

Shaphan prudent, sly; coney, rock badger

Shaphat judge, God has judged

Shapher beautiful, fair; pleasantness, beauty, elegance; [The station of Israel in the wilderness]

Sharai Jah is deliverer; free

Sharaim (same as *Shaaraim*)

Sharar strong, firm

Sharezer (God) protect the king
Sharon [c] a plain, level
Sharuhen [c] dwelling of grace
Shashai noble, free; pale; [One could speculate that in countries where the predomi-nant skin colour was dark, the 'pale' people were likely to be freemen, if not of noble birth].
Shashak assaulter, runner; [activity?]
Shaul asked, asked for; (see *Saul*)
Shaveh [c] level place; plain
Shaveh-kiriathaim plain of Kiriathaim, plain of the double city
Shavsha nobility, splendor, dominion; [could be related to Akkadian *samsu*, the sun-god, or another name for *Seraiah*]
Sheal petition, request, prayer, asking (from God)
Shealtiel I asked from God, I have asked God
Sheariah Jah is decider, gate of Jah, Jah has estimated
Shear-jashub the remnant returns, a remnant shall return; [a symbolic name given to a son of Isaiah (the prophet) before the Syrians and the Ephraimites invaded Judah].
Sheba [c] an oath, abundance or seven; covenant
Shebah an oath, seven
Shebam [c] balsam, fragrance; (same as *Sibmah*)
Shebaniah Jah is powerful; whom Jah hides; ["return, O God"?]
Shebarim [c] breaches, breakings, quarries
Sheber breach, breaking, [Hebrew *seber* = lion; Aramaic *shabra* = childish, simple]
Shebna youthfulness; (shortened *Shebaniah*?)
Shebuel God is renown, captive of God, "Return, O God!"
Shec(h)aniah Jah dwells, Jah is a neighbour, Jah has established his dwelling
Shechem [c] shoulder, back; (see *Sichem*)
Shedeur shedder of light, giving forth of light, Shaddai is light, the Almighty is light

sheep symbolize thoughts; [the symbol is derived from Zodiac, the sign of Ram, during which period we were to have learned control over our thoughts]

Shehariah Jah is the dawn, Jah seeks

Shelah 1. javelin; 2. peace; petition; [also given as possibly: a shoot, a sprout and as 3. an aqueduct]

Shelemiah Jah is recompense, whom Jah repays, Jah has recompensed (or has kept peace, or has completed)

Sheleph ancestor, brother in law; drawn out, drawing out

Shelesh might; triad; obedient, meek; [Consider the might derived from the triad of Is-Ra-El, which is the result of obedience to the dictates of one's Higher Self: El].

Shelomi Jah is peace; peaceful, perfect, peace

Shelomith, Shelomoth peacefulness; (feminine form of the preceding)

Shelumiel God is (my) peace; friend of God

Shem name, fame, renown; [Noah's son of this name symbolizes our physical consciousness, the body].

Shema [c] (God) hears, he (God) has heard, fame, repute

Shemaah the fame, report, (God) has heard

Shemaiah Jah is fame, Jah has heard

Shemariah Jah guards, whom Jah guards, Jah has guarded (or kept preserved)

Shemeber mighty name, splendor of heroism; [soaring on high?]

Shemer watch, watchman, guardian

Shemida(h) fame of knowing, fame of wisdom, my name (or posterity) has known, (the Phoenician god) Eshmun has known (or cared).

Sheminith the eighth, the octave

Shemiramoth fame of the highest, name of heights, most high name

Shemuel (same as *Samuel*)

Shen [c] peak, tooth, a jagged rock

Shenazar (Akkadian:) O Sin (moon-god) protect.

Shenir, Senir peak; snow; coat of mail; (see *Senir*)

Shepham [c] fruitful; nakedness

Shephatiah Jah is judge, whom Jah defends, Jah has judged

shepherd symbolizes one who has (or make an effort to have) conscious control over one's thoughts; (see *sheep*)

Shephi, Shepho baldness, bare, smooth; unconcern

Shephuphan serpent, cerastes or horned snake

Sherah blood-relationship, consanguinity, kinswoman, a female relative

Sherebiah heat of Jah, Jah has parched (or sent burning heat); Jah is originator

Sheresh union; root

Sherezer (same as *Sharezer*)

Sheshach secure habitation; pride; arrogance; [A symbolic name for Babel, or Babylon, alluding to its iron gates or idols]

Sheshai free, noble; [clothed in white?]

Sheshan free noble; [lily? whitish?]

Sheshbazzar fire worshiper; joyous vintager; joy in tribulation; (elsewhere called Zerubbabel: *shoot of Babylon*)

Sheth tumult, substitute; [other etymological roots offer possibilities of: desolation, exaltation and defiance]

Shethar star, commander, lordship, authority

Shethar-boznai starry splen-dor, bright star, one saving the realm (or domain), causing joy, to exalt

Sheva self-satisfying, vanity, like (the father), equal, similar

Shibboleth a stream, torrent, a flood; an ear of corn (or grain), a bunch of twigs

Shibmah [c] balsam, fragrant; [Arabian *shabima* = to be cold]

Shicron [c] fruitfulness; drunkenness

Shiggaion erring; irregular; [dirge? lament?]

Shigionoth (same as preceding)

Shihon [c] heaps of ruins; ruin

Shihor lake or pool of Horus, black; (see *Sihor*)

Shihor-libnath glass river, turbid stream (or swamp) of Libnath

Shilhi a warrior, one with darts; darter

Shilhim [c] fountains; aqueducts

Shillem recompense, requital, he (God) has made compensation

Shiloah sending forth; outlet of water, a sending of waters, an aqueduct; (same as *Siloah*)

Shiloh rest, at ease, the rest giver, peace giver; [A description of Messiah as the Prince of Peace – or as the *seed* of Judah]

Shiloh [c] place of tranquility; [The name of a "city", thus of a state of consciousness implying the preceding]

Shilshah triad might, heroism; [this could be a reference to the symbolic triad of Is-Ra-El] (see *Israel*)

Shimea fame, famous, rumour; (God) has heard (prayer for a child)

Shimeah Jah has heard, splendor, fame; (see preceding)

Shimeam fame, rumour; (see preceding)

Shimeath fame; (see preceding)

Shimei, Shimi, Shimhi Jah is fame, my fame, Jah has heard

Shimeon hearing, a hearkening (of prayer), answering (of prayers for a child), (God) has heard

Shimma rumour, fame; (see *Shimea*)

Shimon trier, valuer; (see *Shimeon*)

Shimrath watch, watching, guarding (by God), watchfulness

Shimri, Simri Jah is watching, watchful, Jah has watched

Shimrith watch, watching (by God), vigilant

Shimrom watch, watching, watch-post

Shimron (same as preceding)

Shimshai Jah is splendor; sunny, my sun, sun-child

Shinab (the moon-god) Sin is (my or his) father; father's tooth; sharpened desire; father of change; father of transgression [hostile?] (see *moon*)

Shinar divided stream; two rivers; divided mind; [symbolizes the state of confusion (or belief in mental limitations)] (see *Babel*)

Shiphi Jah is fulness, abundant, abundance

Shiphrah beauty

Shiphtan judge, judicial, judgement

Shisha distinction, nobility, brightness; alabaster

Shishak illustrious; [MBD offers: present of a bag or pot; like a river]

Shitrai Jah is deciding; official, [officer?]

Shittim [c] acacias (trees)

Shiza (God) has delivered; splendor; [cheerful?]

Shoa rich, opulent, noble

Shobab returning, apostate, deserter, rebellious

Shobach expansion, pouring

Shobai Jah is glorious; God returns, comes back; captivating; returning; [bright? prisoner? one who carries away captives?]

Shobal wandering; stream; basket

Shobek free; forsaker; one who precedes, victor

Shobi Jah is glorious; taking captive

Shoco, Shochoh [c] (see *Socoh*)

Shoham leek-green beryl; onyx; a carnelian

Shomer watcher, watchman, guard

Shophach (same as *Shobach* and/or *Shobek*)

Shophan [c] nakedness, baldness; (or see *Atroth-Shophan*)

Shoshannim lilies, (a Psalm title)

Shoshannim Eduth lilies, a testimony, (a Psalm title)

Shua prosperity, wealth, help, [(God is) help?]

Shuah prosperity; depression

Shual jackal, fox

Shubael (same as *Shebuel*)

Shuham depression; sinking; humility; desperation; well digger; pitman.

S

Shunem [c] uneven; two resting places
Shuni fortunate; quiet
Shupham (see *Shephuphan*)
Shuppim (pertaining to the preceding)
Shur wall; [Note that *Shur* is the name of a desert]
Shushan [c] lily; [Hebrew name for the city of Susa]
Shushan eduth lily of the testimony, (see *Shoshannim eduth*)
Shuthelah setting of Telah: noise of breaking; roar of frenzy; crash of rupture
Sia congregation, assembly
Siaha congregation, council; (same as *Sia*)
Sibbec(h)ai Jah is intervening, entangling
Sibboleth (same as *Shibboleth*)
Sibmah [c] (same as *Shibmah*)
Sibraim [c] double hill; [two hills?]
Sichem [c] ridge, shoulder; the shoulder-blade; (see *Shechem*)
Siddim [c] border furrows, extension, the plains; [salt of salt flats?]; (The shores of the Salt Sea where Sodom, Gomorrah, Admah and Zeboim once were)
Sidon fortified; fishing; (see *Zidon*)
sign symbolizes a "demonstration" i.e. physical evidence of the action of spirit, or the evidence of the efficacy of our prayers. Thus a sign that comes from the "East" is manifested in the "South". (Also see *Zodiac*)
Sihon great, bold; brush
Sihor turbid, slimy; black; [Also called the "river of Egypt"].
Silas [a shorter form of *Silvanus* or from Aramaic: *She'îla*, equivalent to Hebrew *Sha'ûl* = Saul]
Silla highway
Siloah, Siloam (see *Shiloah*)
Silvanus of the forest
Simeon (same as *Shimeon*)
Simon (same as preceding)

Simri (see *Shimri*)

Sin cliff, place; clay; (also the Akkadian moon-god)

sin In the New Testament the Greek word *hamartia* or *hamartano* originates from the sport of archery. Its literal meaning is *missing the mark*.

Sina (Greek form of *Sinai*)

Sinai cliffs; pointed; (Akkadian *Sin* = moon-god)

single eye (see *eye*)

Sinim Far East; the Chinese. [Or from "the land of Syene", the southernmost city of ancient Egypt?]

Sinite miry; muddy; hataful passions; bloodshed; rage; (A tribe of Canaanites, not of the Sinim)

Sion 1.projecting; lifted up, (a peak of Mount Hermon, also called Sirion and Shenir). 2. Greek name for Zion

Siphmoth [c] fruitful; the one with a beard; [bare places?]

Sippai Jah is preserver; threshold, [belonging to the doorstep?]

Sirah (cistern of) turning aside, withdrawing, rebellion, cistern of the thorn-bush

Sirion a coat of mail, cuirass (i.e. a breastplate made of leather); [name given by Sidonians to Mount Hermon in Deuteronomy 3:9]

Sisamai Jah is distinguished; [fragrant? Pertaining to a Phoenician deity called Sasam?]

Sisera mediation, array; [binding in chains?]

Sitnah hatred, contention, accusation, enmity

Sivan bright; [The 3rd month of the Hebrew year, from the new moon of May or June]

six number "6" is symbolic of labour, particularly work without fulfilment. Note that the six-pointed Star of David represents the Old Testament, while the New Testament expresses seven, or the movement from the 'Law' to 'Grace'. [In the Revelation, "666" symbolizes ongoing 'abortive' work].

skull (the) symbolizes the intellect. (see *forehead*)

Smyrna [c] myrrh; aromatic

So chief; prince; crododile; Saturn; (Hebrew form of an
    Egyptian name of a king of Ethiopian descent).
Socoh, Socho [c] a hedge of thorns; (same as *Shocho(h)*)
Sodi my confidant, Jah determines, my intimate council (is
    Jah), an acquaintance
Sodom, Sodoma [c] place of lime; burning; consuming
    with fire; secret intrigues; covered conspiracies;
    [Revelation 11:8, equates Sodom with Egypt and with:
    "where also our Lord was crucified"]
Sodomite separate, set apart
soles (of feet) may symbolize past lives
Solomon peace, peaceable, welfare, well-being
son symbolizes: 1. the outcome of a mental process, e.g. a
    (new) idea; 2. the result or a consequence of an action;
    (see *children*)
son of man symbolizes the human personality; [Son of
    man, with **S** capitalized symbolizes One in whom the
    human consciousness is already redeemed].
Sophereth learning; (female) scribe
Sorek vineyard, choice vine (or grape), bright-red
Sotai Jah is turning aside; deviator
[Soul] This reference in not used in the Bible and is offered
    only to clear up any possible semantic confusion about
    'Soul' (with capitalized S, as against 'soul', given
    below. If the word Soul is used in any part of the
    Dictionary it is always understood to mean the
    Individualization of the One Consciousness (God)
    Note: individual (from Latin *individualis*) means
    indivisible, inseparable. Thus this Divine Spark within
    us, variously referred to as the Christ, the I AM, the
    Higher Self, the Soul (with capitalized S) is an
    integral, inseparable part of the One God. In the Bible,
    it manifests Itself as the unifying principle: *El*.
soul (1) Most commonly used is the Hebrew word *nephesh*
    meaning animal soul i.e. psyche. It symbolizes the
    interaction between the subconscious mind and the

emotions, comprising the personality; (2) The Hebrew *nedibah* (Job 30:15) means: willing, liberal or noble one; (3) The Hebrew word *neshamah* (Isa.57:16) means *breath*; (4) The Greek word *psuchè* or psyche, translated in the New Testament as *soul* is self evident, (it corresponds to the Hebrew *nephesh*). [N.B.: soul is not the divine part of our being. The divine part is the I AM, the individualization of Spirit; (see preceding)]

South The word *south* is liberally ally translated from Hebrew and Greek to mean: the south country or wind, the right hand, pasture land, wilderness, the country of Judah, midday, etc. Symbolically it represents the power of physical manifestation, i.e. the demonstration of the efficacy of one's belief system

Spirit symbolizes the indestruc-tible substance of the manifested universe, the Essence of Life, the source of all Knowledge (see *light*)

Stachys an ear of corn (or grain)

staff symbolizes spiritual support, that which we lean upon when in need of help

stars (of heaven) symbolize our acquired knowledge which we use mind that although the Truth or Divine Knowledge is immutable, our understanding of it increases, thus giving an illusion that a 'new' Truth has been discovered. At an early stage of our evolution (see *Genesis*), stars symbolize the Truth not as yet discovered.

Stephanas crown, crowned, crown-bearer

Stephen (English form of *Stephanas*)

Stoicks [Greek philosophers whose name came from the *Stoa*, a porch in Athens, from which their founder *Zeno* taught severe and lofty pantheism, and indifference (detachment) in all circumstances]

stone, marble etc. The more *noble* materials symbolize the spiritual self. The *base* materials, such as brick, represent the lower self, the human nature.

stronghold (see *fortress*)

Suah riches, distinction; sweepings, rubbish

Succoth booths or huts; [the 1st station of Israel after leaving Rameses in Egypt]

Succoth-benoth booths for the daughters or young women; (one of many Babylonian gods)

Sukkiims nomads; (an African or Egyptian tribe)

Sur turning aside, entrance; (in 2 Chronicles 23:called "gate of the foundation")

Susanna lily, white, bright coloured, ornamental, pure

Susi Jah is swift or rejoicing; horseman, (my) horse

Sychar [c] drunken; [same as *Shechem*?]

Sychem [c] (Greek form of *Shechem*)

Syene [c] opening

Syntyche fortunate (coinci-dence)

Syracuse [c] Tyre hidden; hidden rock; luxurious living; secret; violent drawing; {Gleamed from MBD}

Syria high land

Syrian Aramaic; (The language used in Aram or Syria, similar to Chaldee, as well as the people of the land so named)

T

Taanach [c] battlement; [castle?]

Taanath-shiloh [c] circle of Shiloh; [fig-tree of Shiloh?]

Tabbaoth spots; rings, signet ring

Tabbath [c] extension; pleasantness

Tabeal, Tabeel God is good

Taberah [c] burning; place of feeding

tabernacle tent or dwelling place. [The word symbolizes an early concept of the "temple of the living God", the state of consciousness which manifests as I AM.

Later, in the Promised Land, the more permanent tabernacle is called the Temple of Solomon, i.e. the state of consciousness built on inner peace].

Tabitha gazelle

Tabor mountain height; height

Tab-rimon (the god) Rimmon is good, the deity Ramman is good

Tadmor [c] palms; city of palms

Tahan gracious; camp

Tahapanes [c] head of the land, fortress of Penhase (or of the Negro),

Tahath depression, humility; substitute; (that which is) beneath, compensation; [the 27th station of Israel from Egypt, 11th from Sinai].

Tahpenes wife of a king, [she whom the king protects?] (A queen of Pharaoh, king of Egypt)

Tahrea flight; [cunning?]

Tahtim-hodshi netherlands newly inhabited; lowlands of Hodshi; new foundations; new depths; under the new moon. (see Kadesh)

Talitha girl, maiden; (see *cumi*)

Talmai bold, spirited; [great?]; abounding in furrows, plowman

Talmon oppressor, violentoppressed

Tamah, Thamat combat; joy

Tamar a palm tree, date palms

Tammuz faithful son of the (subterranean, sweet-water) ocean, [son of life?] (A Syrian and Phoenician idol corresponding to the Greek Adonis).

Tanach (see *Taanach*)

Tanhumeth comfort, consolation

Taphath ornament; a drop

Tappuah [c] apple; hill place

Tarah [c] turning, duration, wandering; station; [The 23rd station of Israel from Egypt, 12th from Sinai]

Taralah [c] power of God; reeling; agitating; trembling;

staggering; drunkenness

Tarea flight; (same as *Tahrea*)

Tarshish hard, [or from an Akkadian word meaning: smelting plant or refinery]

Tarsus flat broad surface; flat of foot; wing; blade; flat basket; tranquility; pleasantness; (The birthplace of Paul the Apostle. Tarsus was a noted seat of philosophy and literature, ranking with Athens and Alexandria)

Tartak hero of darkness; for Atargatis; [*Atargatis* is a designation combining the names of two female divinities who were closely associated: *Attar* (or *Astarte*) and *Atta* (*'Anat* to the Canaanites) became *'Atar-'Ate*, or in Greek *Atargatis*. She appears to represent a "mother goddess"]

Tartan military chief; (a title of a commander in chief)

Tatnai gift; dispenser of gifts; reward; rewarder

Tebah thick, strong; (born at the time of) slaughter

Tebaliah Jah is protector; whom Jah has immersed (i.e.: purified), Jah has purified

Tebeth winter; goodness; [The tenth month in Jewish religious year, from the new moon of December or January]

Tehaphnehes (see *Tahapanes*)

Tehinnah supplication, entreaty, cry for mercy

Tekel weighted, to weigh; (see *Mene*)

Tekoa, Tekoah [c] firm, settlement; sound of trumpet, blowing (of alarm)

Tel-abib [c] hill of grass, hill (or heap) of ears of corn (or grain)

Tel-haresha [c] hill of the magus (of silence), forest-hill, mound of artificer (or of enchantment)

Tel-melah [c] hill of salt

Telah fracture, fissure; vigour

Telaim [c] lambs, [with the lambs?]

Telassar Assyrian hill, [hill of Asshur?] (same as

Thelassar)
Telem brightness; a lamb; oppression
Tema sun burnt; a desert; amazement
Teman (one) on the right hand, southern; (see *east*)
Temeni fortunate, a southerner
temple (usually, the "Lord's temple") A state of raised
    consciousness; however when used in conjunction
    with Baal, it represents mental limitation symbolized
    by Baal.
ten number "10" symbolizes the executive faculty;
    (compare: ten horns, ten fingers of our hands, the ten
    commandments, etc.)
Terah 1. in the wilderness, turning, duration, waiting place;
    wandering; [Israel's station in the wilderness on the
    way to Canaan] 2. [ibex?]
Teraphim nourishers, the decaying (or perishing) ones,
    "inert things" [A technical designation for specific
    idols, e.g. household gods (as in Genesis 31:19,34,35
    and later in Judges and Hosea)]
Teresh dry, firm, strictness, reverence, [severe?]
Tertius the third
Tertullus (diminutive of Tertius)
testimony refers to the two tables of the law (the Ten
    Commandments).
Thaddæus breast
Thahash porpoise, dolphin, reddish; [seal?]
Thamah, Tamah combat; laughter
Thamar (Greek form of *Tamar*)
Thara (Greek form of *Terah*)
Tharshish (same as *Tarshish*)
Thebez [c] seen afar; brightness
Thelasar (see *Telassar*)
Theophilus loved by God, friend of God, dear to God
Thimnathah [c] (an assigned or allotted) portion
Thomas a twin; joined; doubled; twain;
thousand years [Psalm 90:3-6] suggests a reference to the

cycles of reincarnation. Plato and Virgil both mention
that a thousand years pass between reincarnations.
This period should not be taken literally, but rather to
denote a very long time. The *Bhagavad-Gita*, for
instance, speaks of an "immensity of years". {For
further reading refer to *Reincarnation, The Phoenix
Fire Mystery*, Compiled and Edited by Joseph Head &
S.L. Cranston, pages 127 and 143.}

three days and... (see *time...*)

Thummim perfection; whole; complete; [truth?] [*Urin* &
    Thummim = lights and perfections]

thunder (and lightning) symbolizes the power of the Word
    of God, i.e. the attention getting call of the Higher
    Self. Also, in addition to "an earthquake" it signifies a
    deeply traumatic experience, taking place in one's
    consciousness.

Thyatira burning insence; inspired; aromatic wood;
    perfume; rushing headlong; (A city of Lydia, once
    called Pelopia and Euhippia. It was famous for the art
    of dying purple).

Tibhath [c] butchery, (place of) slaughter; extension

Tibni intelligent; strawman, [made of straw? (Arabic *tibn*
    = straw)]

Tidal splendor, renown; dread

Tiglath-pileser my trust is in the son of Eshara, [the son of
    the temple of Sarra (or Esharra, the god Ninib) is a
    ground of confidence?] (N.B.: all transliterations have
    been confirmed by the bibliography listed)

Tikvah, Tikvath hope, expectation; strength

Tilgath-pilneser (same as *Tiglath-pileser*)

Tilon mockery, scorn; [gift?]

Timæus highly prized, honorable

time, times and... half time: compare: three *days and a
    half*, (3.5 days = 84 hours i.e. 12 x 7), *forty-two months*
    (3.5 x 12 months), 1260 *days*, (divisible by 12 and by

7), etc.. Whenever the Bible uses numbers to describe
duration, it refers to short, intermediate and long
periods of time. In addition, the figure 12 and 7 figure
prominently. Other than that, the numbers should not
be taken literally, as they bear little if any symbolic
meaning. [As Soul is immortal, time has relatively
little influence on it] (see *twelve, seven* and *Zodiac*)

Timna restraining; unapproachable

Timnah [c] allotment, (allotted) portion (or territory)

Timnath [c] (same as preceding)

Timnath-heres [c] portion of the sun, land dedicated to the
sun, (also see below)

Timnath-serah [c] portion of the remainder; an extra
portion, portion remaining after the division of the
land

Timon honourable, worthy, honoring, reverencing

Timotheus, Timothy honored of God, honoring God, one
who worships (or honors) God

Tiphsah [c] passage, ford

Tiras determination of forms; thought; imagination;
conception; formative faculty;

Tirathite(s) openings; gates; doors; porters; gatekeeper; (a
family of scribes)

Tirhakah exalted; inquirer; beholder; searcher; [distance?]

Tirhanah kindness; [murmuring?]

Tiria Jah is watchful, founda-tion, fear

Tirshatha the reverence (or fear), the revered (or feared)

Tirzah delightfulness, delight, pleasantness, pleasure,
beauty

Titus protected

Toah depression, humility, low; [Akkadian *tahu* = child)

Tob [c] fruitful, good

Tob-adonijah the Lord Jah is good; good is (my) Lord Jah

Tobiah, Tobijah Jah is good

Tochen [c] establishment, measurement, a measure

Togarmah rugged

Tohu humility, depression, low, child; (same as *Toah*)

Toi, Tou error, wandering, wanderer

Tola warm, crimson, scarlet

Tolad [c] place where children could be obtained, begetter, birth

Tophel [c] mortar, lime, whitewash; [a station of Israel in the wilderness]

Tophet [c] altar; burning; [possibly: "spitting out" or "a place of abhorrence", but generally: "a place of burning"]

Tormah privily, treachery, [in secret?]

Tou (see *Toi*)

Trachonitis rugged, rough (or hilly or stony) region; [although not a place one would "abide in", doubtless it refers to a state of consciousness]

tree often symbolizes the 'major' acquests of physical consciousness; [it is that which grows out of the earth] (see *earth* and *grass*)

tribe (s) each *tribe* symbolizes an inherent quality or trait of character to be mastered by our efforts. Only after all the 12 qualities are perfected, we enter into a higher state of consciousness, i.e. the Promised Land. [Compare the predispositions of character ascribed to theZodiac].

Trophimus nourishing, nutritious, [master of the house?]

Tryphena delicate, dainty, luxuriant

Tryphosa (same as preceding)

Tubal [production?]

Tubal-cain Tubal the smith, [producer of weapons?]

twelve number "12" symbolizes all-round (group) completeness; compare: 12 signs of the Zodiac, 12 tribes of Israel, 12 apostles, 12 facets of human character, 12 animals of Buddha etc.. [The origin of the numbers 12 and 7 (see *seven*) reaches back to the ancient concept of the *Wheel of Eighty-Four* (12 x 7), wherein 84 multiplied by 100,000 years (*lakhs*) refers to the number of embodiments in different species through which a soul will pass during its early existence]. (see *Zodiac*)

twenty-four elders symbolize the qualities redeemed during the two previous signs of the Zodiac; (see *Zodiac*)

Tychicus fortunate, fortuitous, happy

Tyrannus tyrant, an absolute ruler

Tyre rock; refuge

Tyrus (Latin name for *Tyre*)

U

Ucal I shall prevail

Uel [perhaps from: *'U'el* = will (or desire) of God; or from *Abuel* = God is a father]

Ulai twisted together; strong; powerful; foremost; ram's horn; leather bottle; (being a river, it symbolizes a *change* in consciousness)

Ulam foremost, first, leader; solidarity

Ulla burden, yoke

Ummah [c] union, kindred, community, close by

unclean (the) symbolize thoughts of limitation (beliefs in limitation)

unclean animals (same as preceding)

Unni Jah has answered, answering is with Jah, depressed; humbeled

U-pharisin and-divided, dividers; (see *Mene*)

Uphaz [c] pure gold; fold region; radiating light; [possibly a corruption of *Ophir*]

Ur [c] (God is) light, brightness

Urbane (Latin **Urbanus**) urbane, refined, pleasant

Uri Jah is my light, Jah is a light; enlightened; fiery; (shortened form of Uriah)

Uriah, Urijah Jah is (my) light, light of Jah
Urias (Greek form of *Uriah*)
Uriel God (El) is (my) light, light of God
Urim lights; enlightenments; [Urim and Thummim =
    "lights and perfection", although since they were
    objects used by priests to determine the will of God,
    the two words could also mean: "light and dark"]
Uthai Jah is help, Jah has shown himself surpassing;
    helpful
Uz firmness; fertile
Uzai Jah has heard; hoped for
Uzal wanderer
Uzza, Uzzah (Jah is) strength
Uzzen-sherah [c] point, top of Sherah, ear of Sheerah
Uzzi Jah is strong, might of Jah, (shortened form of *Uzziah*)
Uzzia, Uzziah (same as preceding)
Uzziel God is my strength, God is strong, power of God

V

Vajezatha born of Ized; strong as the wind; son of
    maturity; white; whitened; white-robed.
valley symbolizes a state of consciousness directly opposite
    that symbolized by a *hill* or *mountain*; it stands for
    fear, confusion, and belief in limitation.
Vaniah Jah is praise worthy of love, lovable; distress.
Vashni Jah is strong; [strong?]
Vashti the desired one, the beloved, the best one; beautiful;
    fair; lovely.
vengeance invariably symbolizes *vindication*
Vophsi rich; my increase; expansion; added unto me.

W

wait upon the Lord symbolizes the desire to intensify spiritual activity

walled city symbolizes a consciousness not willing or able to absorb or entertain new ideas; ("a closed mind").

warrior symbolizes everyone of us as we struggle towards the spiritual consciousness.

wars symbolize battles within one's consciousness: the efforts to control one's thoughts; mental struggles.

water symbolizes human soul [psyche] as represented by the mental movement, i.e. that in which a change of consciousness takes place; (see: *woman* and *moon*)

waters the potential thoughts as yet to be manifested, or made conscious. (see *seas*)

way symbolizes a journey back to God (towards the realization of the omnipresence of God)

weak hand (s) symbolizes the belief in limitation (resulting in one's failure to manifest or demonstrate the results of prayer).

well (s) (see *Beer*)

wicked (the) symbolize negative thoughts (see: *enemies* and *heathen*)

widow symbolizes "the dark night of the soul".

wilderness symbolizes: (1) the inability to realize the Presence of God; (2) a state of consciousness in which we begin to build up a new awareness, develop new concepts; (see *desert, land*)

wind symbolizes the action or the influence of Spirit: (see *breath*)

wine symbolizes secret knowledge.

witnesses (two) symbolize the male and female principles of human nature; (see *olive trees*)

woman symbolizes the soul; the subconscious; (see *soul, water* and *moon*)

woman clothed... *in the sun*: symbolizes a soul which already attained selfrealization, but is still short of God-realization.
word of God symbolizes the Divine Truth
world symbolizes physical consciousness (see *earth*)
wrath same meaning as vengeance, i.e. vindication [from Latin: *vindicatio*, a claiming].

Y

yoke symbolizes the attachment, bondage or enslavement to the limitations of our lower nature [be it physical, emotional or mental].

Z

Zaanaim double migratory tent; load; great migration; exodus; [wanderings?]
Zaanan [c] rich in flocks; place of flocks
Zaanannim (same as *Zaanaim*)
Zaavan, Zavan causing fear, terror; disturbed; [trembling?]
Zabad he (God) bestows, he (God) has given; endower; gift
Zabbai roving about, pure; [he (God) has given?]
Zabbud well remembered, endowed; (God has) given
Zabdi Jah is endower, the gift of Jah, my gift
Zabdiel God is endower, the gift of God, El (God) has given
Zabud endowed; given (or bestowed) by God
Zabulon (Greek form of *Zebulun*)

Zaccai pure, blameless; (or contraction of *Zachariah*)

Zacchæus (Greek form of *Zaccai*)

Zaccur, Zacchur God has remembered, well remembered, mindful

Zachariah Jah is renowned, whom Jah remembers, Jah has remembered

Zacharias (Greek form of the preceding)

Zacher God has remembered; fame; memorial

Zadok righteous; just

Zaham fatness; loathing, putrid, loathsome

Zair [c] little, small

Zalaph caper plant (or bush), purification; breaking forth; wound; hurting

Zalmon, Salmon [c] terrace, ascent; shady, dark; image, likeness (see *Salmon*)

Zalmonah [c] giving shade, shaded, (same as preceding) [The 34th station of Israel from Egypt, the 23rd from Sinai]

Zalmunna withdrawn from protection, shelter denied, shadow (i.e. protection) is withheld, [or, (the god) Salm (i.e. the dark-one) rules]

Zamzummim (s) powerful, vig-orous; rumorers, makers of noise

Zanoah [c] broken district, marsh, repugnance, stench

Zaphnath-paaneah saviour of world, prince of the life of the age, "(god) speaks and (the bearer of the name) lives"

Zaphon [c] north, concealed; (Symbolically, that which is north is concealed)

Zara, Zarah, Zerah dawning, dawn, shining, [sunrise?]; sprout

Zareah [c] stinging, wasp; disease; (also see *Zorah*)

Zared, Zered willow bush; exuberant growth; [elsewhere called: "*brook of the willows*" and "*river of wilderness*"]

Zarephath [c] place of refining; [Akkadian *sariptu* from *sarapu* = to dye)

Zaretan, Zartanah [c] cooling; penetrataing; [great (or lofty) rock?]

Zareth-shahar [c] light of the dawn, the splendor of the morning, brightness of the dawn

Zattu, Zatthu lovely, pleasant; [irascible?]

Zavan (see *Zaavan*)

Zaza projection; glittering; sparkling; emitting splendor; projecting rays; flowering; [fullness?]

zeal (of the Lord) 'zeal' means action; (see *action*)

Zebadiah gift of Jah, Jah is endower, Jah has given (or bestowed); [this is the full form of *Zabdi*]

Zebah (victim of) slaughter, (born on the day of) sacrifice

Zebaim [c] gazelles; (see *Pochereth-hazzebaim*)

Zebedee (Greek form of *Zebadiah*)

Zebina purchased, purchase, bought,

Zeboim, Zeboiim [c] gazelles; waging of wars; plunderings; (one of the five cites in the valley of Siddim, destroyed with Sodom and Gomorrah).

Zeboim [c] wild place; gazelles, hyenas; wild beasts; ravenous appetites; bestiality

Zebudah bestowed (by God), endowed, given

Zebul dwelling, habitation, rulership, dominion; prince, ruler; [all these refer (symbolically) to the control of one's thoughts within one's consciousness]

Zebulun dwelling, habitation; prince, exalted, rulership, dominion; (see preceding)

Zechariah Jah is renowned, whom Jah remembers, Jah has remembered

Zedad [c] side, sloping place; [hunting?]

Zedekiah Jah is might, justice of Jah, Jah is righteous

Zeeb wolf, jackal

Zelah [c] slope; rib side

Zelek split, rent, fissure; an outcry, utter a loud cry

Zelophehad fracture; shadow of fear (i.e. a dreadful shadow or protection against fear)

Zelotes zealous, eager ones, emulators; (Greek: *zelotes* from *zelos* meaning: zeal) [From about 6 A.D., it denoted members of a Jewish sect in open struggle against the Roman rule in Palestine]

Zelzah [c] sun protection, shade in the heat

Zemaraim [c] double peak, double mount forest, two fleeces

Zemira song, praised

Zenan [c] place of (or rich in) flocks; (same as Zaanan)

Zephaniah Jah has concealed (or protected, or hidden, or treasured); Jah is darkness

Zephath [c] watchtower, mountain watch

Zephathah [c] watchtower; (perhaps the same as preceding)

Zephi, Zepho watch

Zephon (God is) watching, lookout, a looking out; dark, wintry

Zer [c] rock; pebble; flint; narrow; compressed; distress; affliction

Zerah, Zarah dawn, dawning, shining; sprout

Zerahiah Jah is appearing, whom Jah caused to rise, Jah has shone forth, Jah has dawned

Zered (see *Zared*)

Zereda(h) [c] the fortress, town; cool, [Arabic: *sard* = cold]

Zeredathah (same as preceding)

Zererath cutting; penetrating; piercing; cold, cooling; (could be a variant of Zeredah)

Zeresh gold; [Avestan: *zarsh* could imply the following: one with dishovelled hair, ruffled one; joyful or elated one]

Zereth splendor, brightness; [gold?]

Zeri balm; resin or mastic tree

Zeror bundle, bag; pebble, sharp stone, flint

Zeruah full breasted; leprous, skin-diseased; stricken

Zerubbabel offspring (or seed or shoot) of Babylon;

scattered in Babylon

Zeruiah perfumed with mastic, balm

Zetham, Zethan olive trees, one working with olive trees; shining

Zethar sacrifice; spendor; brilliance; conqueror; [killer or victor or smiter from Old Persian *jantar* meaning: slayer?]

Zia terrified, trembler; motion

Ziba branch, twig, plantation; planter

Zibeon wild robber; dyed; hyena

Zibia, Zibiah gazelle; roe

Zichri Jah has remembered, renowned, famous, my remembrance

Ziddim [c] sides, the mountain side

Zidkijah (see *Zedekiah*)

Zidon, Sidon [c] fortress; fishing

Zif blossom or flower month; [the 2nd month of the Hebrew year, from the new moon of April or May]

Ziha drought

Ziklag [c] winding, bending

Zillah shadow (i.e.: protection of God), protection, screen, shade

Zilpah myrrh dropping, dropping, [Arabic *zulfah* = dignity]

Zilthai (Zillethai) (Jah is) a shadow, protection, shady

Zimmah (Jah) has considered, council, consideration, purpose; planning

Zimran, Zimri Jah is active (i.e. helpful), celebrated, [my praise is Jah)?]

Zin [c] low land

Zina sharp; pointed; coldness; shield; depression; lowland; low palm. [A wilderness in southern Palestine]

Zion fortress; refuge; sunny; [The southwest hill of Jerusalem, often called the City of David, symbolizes God realization: a state of consciousness, which cannot be attained by own efforts].

Zior [c] smallness, little

Ziph [c] refining place; flowing
Ziphah lent flowing; fluid; flux; pure; refined; clean
Ziphion (same as *Zephon*)
Ziphron [c] beautiful top; sweet smell; to stink
Zippor sparrow, bird
Zipporah swallow, little bird; [feminine form of *Zippor*]
Zithri Jah is protection, my hiding place (is Jah)
Ziz [c] a flower, blossom, ornament; protection
Ziza, Zizah shining, brightness; abundance
Zoan [c] low region; (the capital of Egypt)
Zoar [c] little, small, smallness
Zoba, Zobah [c] encampment; fixed; set in bounds; appointed; a plantation [from Akkadian for: "soaking (fields)"?]
Zobebah the affable; walking slowly; [lizard?]
Zodiac is a powerful symbol throughout the Bible. Every approx. 26,000 years the earth traces an orbit called the Procession of the Equinoxes symbolized by the Zodiac. Each of the 12 "signs" (about 2150 years each) stands for a basic quality of human nature, and during each segment (sign) we are to learn our relationship to God through the development of that particular quality. (see *twelve*)
Zohar nobility, distinction; light, tawny, fawn color (i.e. yellowish-red) [It is evident that at least some of the scholars equate the lightness of (skin) color with distinction if not nobility]
Zoheleth serpent or gliding or creeping; serpent stone
Zoheth proud, corpulent, strong
Zophah bellied jar or jug; watch; [a curse?]
Zophai watcher; honeycomb
Zophar hairy, rough; chatterer, chirper, twitter
Zophim [c] watchers, watchmen
Zorah, Zareah [c] prominent; wasp, a place of hornets; disease
Zorobabel (Greek form of *Zerubbabel*)

Zuar little, small

Zuph honeycomb (see Zophai); flag, sedge

Zur rock

Zuriel God (El) is a (or my) rock, God is the rock

Zuri-shaddai the (Shaddai) Almighty is a rock, whose Almighty is a rock

Zuzims strong people or nations, prominent, sparkling, glittering; strong, giant

***

BIBLIOGRAPHY

Bromiley, Geoffrey W., (General editor) *The International Standard Bible Encyclopedia.* [© 1979 by William B. Eerdmans Publishing Co. *A Complete Concordance to the Old and New Testaments.* © MDCCCLIV Alexander Gruden M.A., London James Dinnis]

Campbell, Joseph *The Hero with a Thousand Faces*, [©1949 by Bollingen Foundation Inc., New York, N.Y.] pg. 236

Fox, Emmet *Diagrams for Living*, [©1968 by Harper and Row, Publishers, 10 East 53rd Street, New York, N.Y. 10022]

Fox, Emmet *Alter your Life*, © 1932 – 1950 by Emmet Fox, Published by Harper and Row, 10 East 53rd Street, New York, N.Y. 10022

Fox, Emmet *Power through Constructive Thinking*, © 1932–1940 by Emmet Fox, Published by Harper and Row, New York, Hagerstown, San Francisco.

Hastings M.A., D.D., James, Editor *A Dictionary of the Bible* (first impression 1900, third June 1902). Published in Edinburgh by T.&T. Clark, 38 George Street, and in New York, by Charles Scribner's sons, 153-157 Fifth Avenue. (4 volumes)

Horn Ph.D., Siegfried H. *Seventh-Day Adventist Bible Dictionary* [© 1960, 1979 by the Review and Herald Publishing Assoc.]

Jung, Carl G. (edited by) *Man and his Symbols*, ©1964 Aldus Books Ltd. London.

Kapuscinski, Stanislaw *Beyond Religion vol. I.* [© by Stanislaw Kapuscinski 1997. Published by Inhousepress, Montreal, Canada 1998, 2001, 2002]

Kapuscinski, Stanislaw *Key to Immortality, a Commentary on the Gospel of Thomas,* [© by Stanislaw Kapuscinski 1998. Published by Inhousepress, Montreal, Canada 2002]

Metaphysical Bible Dictionary printed by the Unity School of Christianity, Unity Village, Mo. U.S.A. [Compiled and published in 1931: "It is one of the basic books containing Charles Fillmore's inspired teaching..."]

Myers, Allen C., Revision Editor, *The Eerdmans Bible Dictionary*, [©1987 by Wm. B. Eerdman's Publishing Co.]

Pagels, Elaine *The Gnostic Gospels*, [© 1979 by Elaine Pagels; published by Vintage Books 1981, A Division of Random House, New York]

Strong S.T.D., LL.D., James *The Exhaustive Concordance of the*

Bible. Abington, Nashville © 1890 by James Strong, Madison N.J.

The Holy Bible, King James Version, [published by Thomas Nelson Inc. Camden, New Jersey]

The Gospel According to Thomas; Coptic text established and translated by A Guillaumont, H.-Ch. Puech, G. Quispel, W. Till and Yassah 'Abd Al Masih. © E.J. Brill 1959. [Published by Leiden E.J Brill, Harper & Row, New York and Evanston]

Webster's New Twentieth Century Dictionary - Unabridged, Second Edition, [© 1975 by William Collins + World Publishing Co., Inc.]

Young, LL.D., Robert, *Analytical Concordance to the Bible* [Published by Wm. B. Eerdmans Publishing Company, Grand Rapids, Michigan]

Acknowledgments

The *Metaphysical Bible Dictionary* came to me only some ten years after I finished writing my own Dictionary of Biblical Symbolism. Rather than changing the entries that I had already compiled from great many sources, I took the liberty of adding only such items that were missing from my original work. For this opportunity I am very grateful to the late Charles Fillmore and all the people who must have worked with him. I can gladly recommend the *MBD* to all serious students of metaphysics. I am obviously as grateful to the authors of all my other sources, alas, most of them are also no longer alive. It is to all of them that I dedicate my own efforts.

Finally, I must stress, again, that I am *not* a biblical scholar. I looked far and wide for a document that might explain to me the symbolism of the Bible. All to no avail. Since reading books authored by Emmet Fox I have been deeply dissatisfied with professional scholars' interpretation of the Scriptures. I began my long search. Some twenty years later I finished this work which, in a way, will never be finished. I hope, however, that those who seek to unveil the mysteries of the scriptures will find my efforts of some help.

A Word about the Author

Stanislaw Kapuscinski (aka **Stan I.S. Law**), architect, sculptor, and prolific writer, was educated in Poland and England. Since 1965 he has resided in Canada. His special interests cover a broad spectrum of arts, sciences, and philosophy. His fiction and non-fiction attest to his particular passion for the scope and the development of human potential. He authored more than twenty-five books, fifteen of them novels. His short stories, 'literary', though tending towards Visionary-Science-Fiction, have been published extensively.

Under his real name he published seven non-fiction books sharing his vision of reality. He also composed two collections of poems in his original native tongue in which he satirizes his view of the world while paying homage to Bozena Happach's sculptures.

By the same Author (Stan I.S. Law),

Novels
Published by **Inhousepress**
(Most available on the Amazon)

YESHUA—Personal Memoir of the Missing Years of Jesus
PETER & PAUL Intuitive sequel to YEASHUA
ONE JUST MAN [Winston Trilogy Book I)
ELOHIM—Masters & Minions [Winston Trilogy Book II]
WINSTON'S KINGDOM [Winston Trilogy Book III)
THE PRINCESS [Alexander Trilogy Book I]
ALEXANDER [Alexander Trilogy Book II]
SACHA—The Way Back [Alexander Trilogy Book III]
ENIGMA OF THE SECOND COMING
GIFT OF GAMMAN
NOW—BEING AND BECOMING
THE AVATAR SYNDROME
[Prequel to the *Headless World—The Vatican Incident*]
HEADLESS WORLD—The Vatican Incident
[Sequel to *The Avatar Syndrome*]
THE GATE—Things My Mother Told Me
MARVIN CLARK—In Search of Freedom

Short stories
THE JEWEL
CATS AND DOGS
SCI-FI 1
SCI-FI 2

Poetry in Polish
KILKA SŁÓW I TROCHĘ GLINY
WIĘCEJ SŁÓW I WIĘCEJ GLINY

DICTIONARY of Biblical Symbolism
is also available on Amazon Kindle.

Made in the USA
Columbia, SC
08 August 2020

15846011R00128